YOUR
DIGITAL
Afterlife

When Facebook, Flickr and Twitter Are Your Estate,
What's Your Legacy?

New Riders | VOICES THAT MATTER™

For more information and resources vist www.yourdigitalafterlife.com

Your Digital Afterlife:
When Facebook, Flickr and Twitter Are Your Estate, What's Your Legacy?
Evan Carroll and John Romano

New Riders
1249 Eighth Street
Berkeley, CA 94710
510/524-2178
510/524-2221 (fax)

Find us on the Web at: www.newriders.com
To report errors, please send a note to errata@peachpit.com
New Riders is an imprint of Peachpit, a division of Pearson Education.

Project Editor: Michael J. Nolan
Development Editor: Margaret S. Anderson
Production Editor: Cory Borman
Copyeditor: Gretchen Dykstra
Proofreader: Doug Adrianson
Indexer: Joy Dean Lee
Cover Designer: Charlene Charles Will
Interior design and composition: Kim Scott, Bumpy Design

ISBN 13: 978-0-321-73228-6
ISBN 10:   0-321-73228-6

9 8 7 6 5 4 3 2

Printed and bound in the United States of America

For everyone who lives the digital lifestyle.

Acknowledgements

It takes more than a pair of authors to write and publish a book. We would like to send our heartfelt thanks to the people who supported us throughout the process:

John's wife, **Christina**, and his son, **Nikolas**, for being awesome. Thanks also to his **Mom** and **Dad** for teaching him what's important.

Evan's **Mom** and **Dad**, his sister**, Becky**, and his entire family for their encouragement and patience.

Virginia Ingram for setting us on our path and always encouraging us.

Omar Gallaga for his most excellent foreword and support.

Michael Nolan for believing in the value of our book and helping us make it happen.

Margaret Anderson for her guidance as our development editor.

Nathan Dosch for his expert legal review.

Nancy Aldrich-Ruenzel and the entire **Peachpit staff** for bringing the book to life.

Rich Evers for providing the introductions that made this book possible.

Hugh Forrest and the **SXSW staff** for helping us bring this issue to a larger stage.

Jim Doughty for lending his mastery of words to our title.

Paul Smith for supporting us and having a most generic name to use (or abuse) as an example.

Bruce DeBoer and **Britt Brown** for their photographic talents.

Babatola Oguntoyinbo for listening to Evan's rants from time to time.

John Ellsworth and family for their enthusiasm.

John's **Uncle Grant** for sharing his letters with the world.

Matt Haughey for sharing more about Brad Graham's wonderful story.

Our employer, **Capstrat,** for surrounding us with smart, talented people.

...and to the countless other friends and family members who provided encouragement and didn't mind us talking about death all the time.

Thanks again,
John and Evan

CONTENTS

SECURING YOUR DIGITAL LEGACY

FOREWORD

By Omar L. Gallaga

In March 2009, the authors of *Your Digital Afterlife* co-presented a "Core Conversation" at the South by Southwest (SXSW) Interactive Festival called "Who Will Check My Email After I Die?" Core Conversations are stripped-down panels with only one or two speakers and lots of audience participation. By all accounts, the discussion, which was also facilitated by entrepreneur Matt Ludwig, was a huge success. It generated enthusiastic chatter from several people I was following on Twitter, was the jumping-off point for several great blog entries on the subject of the digital afterlife, and was even mentioned on the NPR segment I contribute to, "All Tech Considered."

Omar L. Gallaga
Photo: Mark Matson, Austin American-Statesman

I missed it.

You have to understand, SXSW Interactive lasts five days and, as a local tech reporter, I try to cover it like a huge, stretched-out, hard-working blanket. The Core Conversation was held at 5 p.m. on Tuesday, the last day of the festival, and by that point I was a threadbare, tattered sheet of a man. As I blogged away on my laptop and saw that the time was drawing near for the last slot of the last set of panels of the fest, I decided to stay put in the luxurious, very fun Blogger's Lounge. A newspaper colleague of mine was already covering the panel and, I thought to myself, if the session were going to be that great, why would they stick it in that slot? It was, poetically, *an actual death slot*. I mean, come on. *Come on.*

Also, they were serving beer in the Blogger's Lounge.

One year later, two discussions on death and digital data were held in that same regrettable SXSW Interactive death slot, but this time I made sure to attend. There's nothing like living with deep regret for twelve months to encourage better decision making.

And speaking of regret...the book you hold in your hands (or are reading in electronic form) is a big ball of warnings and solutions to a set of problems that is looming large in every one of our lives. Death, inevitable, is coming for each of us, but what happens to all the data we consume and create is a question that has never been harder to answer.

Just as it's hard to care about doing regular backups for your computer until data disaster strikes, nobody enjoys thinking about where all our emails, MP3s, Facebook profiles, and tweets will end up when we go to what the TV show *Lost* might call, "The Great Sideways." (Retroactive spoiler there. Sorry.) One thing's for sure: That data doesn't just go away, as much as we'd like it to, when we are gone. And it isn't all just freely available to family members who might seek to preserve your digital legacy.

Death, inconvenient, brings with it many thorny problems in regard to privacy, ownership, and your data's value, in both sentimental and monetary measures. What exactly is a high-level World of Warcraft account worth to a deceased player's family? Should the contents of emails belonging to a soldier killed in action be bequeathed to a spouse or parents? Are there things you can do to plan ahead or should you rely on the many companies that have sprung up to help you deal with digital death details?

Luckily, you don't have to navigate the choppy legal waters or debate the moral questions around these issues; Evan Carroll and John Romano have done that for you. They offer in this book not only stories of grief-stricken people affected by these issues, but practical ways to protect your legacy and to deal with the terms of service for popular online services should you ever be in the terrible position of caretaking a loved one's digital dynasty.

It's good information you won't want to miss the way I did the first time around.

Omar L. Gallaga is a technology culture reporter for the Austin American-Statesman, *where he also writes on the blog* Digital Savant. *He's a contributor to NPR's "All Tech Considered" segments and has written for CNN.com,* The Wall Street Journal, *MSNBC.com, and* Hispanic *magazine. His own blog is at Terribly-Happy.com.*

CHAPTER 1

INTRODUCING THE DIGITAL AFTERLIFE

Email, photos, videos, Facebook accounts—they're the elements of your new digital life. In fact, almost without realizing it, we have shifted toward an all-digital culture. Future heirlooms like family photos, home movies, and personal letters are now created and stored in digital form. And increasingly they're stored online at popular sites that might not be accessible to your loved ones after you pass away.

But in the mad rush to embrace the digital lifestyle, you may have neglected to ask:

" **What happens to my digital stuff when I die?** "

It's an important question. Unfortunately there's not a definite, clear, or simple answer. It's easy to assume that your digital possessions will always be there, but they're not as safe as you might think. There are numerous technical and legal issues that could cause their demise. If you don't take steps to make them available to your loved ones, your digital legacy could be lost forever.

You should realize that there's a cost to not taking action. In effect, you're letting whatever may happen, happen. We're sure that you have some ideas about what should happen to your digital things (and if you don't now you will before the end of this book). But if you don't take action, your wishes are just that: wishes. There's no guarantee or hope that they will be carried out.

But you can stop that from happening. We're here to explain this radical new shift to a digital life, how it relates to your legacy, and what you can do about it.

Why Is This Happening?

This uncertain future for your digital assets is the result of the huge shift that's taking place. We are rapidly moving from physical to digital objects. Photos, letters, movies, documents, books, music—everything—is going digital. This means that old communication mediums are quickly moving aside. Things like family photo albums, stacks of letters, and film reels are casualties of this shift. While the improvements to our devices and media are progress, we should pause and consider what we've lost and what we've gained.

You're Living the Digital Lifestyle

You may not think of yourself as someone who's living the digital life-style, but here's betting it's been years since you used a film camera. Statistics show that you own a phone that can text, email, and browse the Web. They also indicate that an increasing part of your life is lived online. While these changes seem inconsequential on the surface, the total effect is that digital technology is transforming the daily experience of life.

Technology Is Evolving at a Breakneck Pace

Mobile devices are now ubiquitous and we're connected everywhere. New devices and even new methods of connecting are emerging almost daily. We can create and share content in an instant. As a result, there's a content explosion happening on the Web—and a portion of that content belongs to you. You're creating, collecting, and sharing a staggering amount of content every day, right from the palm of your hand. That's adding up quickly, probably more quickly than you realize.

Your Content Is a Reflection of You

All this content forms a rich collection that reflects who you are and what you think. Whether you realize it or not, that makes it quite valu-able. When others respond with a comment or retweet, they're adding value to your collection. As more family photos, home movies, and email messages are created, the entire collection becomes a fuller reflection of you and thus more valuable, both to you and the people you share it with.

Your Content Is Your Legacy

However morbid it may seem, death is certain. When you pass away you will leave behind your digital content. Taken as a whole, this content is your digital legacy. Passing this legacy on will become more important as the shift to digital continues and as your digital content becomes a richer reflection of you.

But there's also a huge opportunity that's never been available to ordinary people—a permanent archive of your life that could exist beyond your physical life. While the Internet can't make you immortal, with a little planning, your legacy could have a glorious afterlife.

Your Digital Legacy Is at Risk

As it stands right now, your digital legacy is at risk of extinction. Our society is creating and storing digital content without much thought to its long-term availability. We're entering a time when it's essential to consider the digital assets of the deceased. We have to address new challenges surrounding digital files such as awareness, access, ownership, and preservation. Unfortunately the process for dealing with these digital assets is still up in the air as we don't yet have sufficient laws or social customs to help us through.

Finding a Solution

With many of the new challenges brought about by digital assets still unaddressed, the responsibility is on you to address them. Whether you're a casual email user or a digital dweller who can't do anything without tweeting about it, you should take steps to secure your digital legacy.

The good news is that those steps are well within reach. With a bit of understanding and planning, you can address the challenges head on. And we wrote this book to help you do just that.

The book is divided into two parts. In the first half, we'll look at how digital technology affects us during our lives and at death and what happens next. We'll introduce you to the risks your digital legacy will face and current advances that will help you circumnavigate them. In the second half, we'll walk you through a practical step-by-step process to help secure your assets. You'll start by making an inventory of them, and deciding upon your wishes for each. Then we'll help you create a plan to leave them behind for the next generation and perhaps for posterity.

Now let's jump in. There's a lot of ground to cover, but we think you'll enjoy the ride.

We all die. The goal isn't to live forever, the goal is to create something that will.

—CHUCK PALAHNIUK

Your Digital Life, Death, and Beyond

Quotation on page 6 from Diary: A Novel *by Chuck Palahniuk*

CHAPTER 2

THE SHIFT TO DIGITAL

News from the Front

In 1968 John's uncle, Grant Wilson, was drafted into the US Army and sent to Vietnam. They put him in the infantry, gave him an M16, and assigned him to a mortar team. His assignments at firebases around Vietnam made it impossible for him to call home, so he sent letters to talk about what he was experiencing and to reassure the family that he was safe.

Grant Wilson in Vietnam in 1968.

Photo courtesy of Grant Wilson

The letters were handwritten by Grant. They are now yellowed by time and have that strange old-paper smell. Some are smeared with mud from the monsoon season. In the letters Grant occasionally wrote about mortar attacks and the enemy, but he wrote at great length about food, mud, bunkers, mustaches, and the care packages he received. Sometimes he sent along a roll of film to be developed. Other times he reflected on current events, like he did on July 20, 1969, as he wrote, "How about those ASTRONAUTS!!" on the back of an envelope as Neil Armstrong was stepping foot onto the moon.

Grant's letters from Vietnam.
Photo by Britt Brown

Grant's sister, Sue, kept these letters, and received each one with the knowledge that it might be the last she heard from her brother. Their content was less important than the fact that their arrival meant that Grant was alive and well. Each one brought a sigh of relief and a hope that her brother might come home alive.

In April 1970, 35 letters and one year later, Grant boarded a military transport plane and flew home to his family. After picking him up at the airport, Sue boxed the letters up and stored them safely in the closet.

Looking at them now, these letters have become personal artifacts that connect Grant and Sue to each other and to the broader history of the United States. It is little wonder that she kept them safely tucked away for the past 40 years.

Let's jump ahead 35 years to another soldier, US Marine Justin Ellsworth. Justin was sent to Iraq to conduct security and stabilization operations in Al Anbar province. His job was to find and defuse the deadly improvised explosive devices, or IEDs, that the insurgency used against American troops. Justin knew that his work kept other soldiers safe and he carried out his duties faithfully.

Much had changed about communications between the time when Grant was in Vietnam and the time when Justin was in Iraq, most dramatically the advent of the Internet. Instead of letters, Justin exchanged emails with his father, John Ellsworth. At times they were able to connect via a telephone call, instant message, or video chat, but the time difference made email much more convenient. John would often share the emails with the whole family. These emails, just like Grant's letters, were a source of comfort for everyone. Justin also received supportive emails in return and he made plans to create a scrapbook of them upon his return.

Justin Ellsworth in Iraq.
Photo courtesy of John Ellsworth

Justin and his father also exchanged photographs, particularly of sunsets, an interest that they shared. In October 2004 John emailed his son a photo of a sunset over a lake nearby their favorite camping spot and asked him to "beat that sunset."

Justin beat that sunset with a photo of one over the Euphrates River with Fallujah in the background. That photo came in an email from a gunnery sergeant who had found it on a CD marked "for Dad" among Justin's belongings after he was killed defusing a roadside IED on November 13, 2004.

Subject: **Somewhere in Iraq**
From: Justin Ellsworth
Date: October 16, 2004 3:25 AM EST
To: John Ellsworth

Hello all! today is oct. 16 and there has been alot going on as i am sure you all have seen on the news. i just wanted to let you all know that i am still alive and well! and missing you all very much. i love looking at every ones pictures! i wish i could be there for the holidays. i remember the halloween hay rides were always so much fun. i bet the wagon will be quite full if you all do it this year. i cant wait to see the pictures! well i should go. i love you all and i cant wait to see you again! i will try to send michelle and yann some pictures of my self do what i do over here. i hope to see you all soon.

Love Justin

An email that Justin Ellsworth sent while he was in Iraq.
Courtesy of John Ellsworth

The emails between Justin and his father didn't take weeks to deliver like Grant's letters. They were delivered instantly across the globe. Their lack of physical form didn't mean they were of any less comfort to Justin's friends and family. In many respects these communications, Justin's emails and Grant's letters, were very much the same.

But there was an important difference. A difference that would later cause Justin's father a good deal of frustration. Unlike Grant's letters, Justin's emails were subject to the terms of service (or legalese) of his email provider.

After his funeral, Justin's family decided to obtain all the emails Justin had received. They wanted to make the scrapbook that Justin had intended to put together when he returned. But Yahoo, Justin's email provider, blocked the request and wouldn't grant the family access to Justin's account. Yahoo cited a clause in its terms of service, which stated that their accounts were *non-transferable*.

Dismayed by Yahoo's policy, John took the issue to court, both the court of public opinion and the Probate Court of Oakland County, Michigan. The issue gained national attention and, after six months, a judge signed an order instructing Yahoo to provide John with copies of his son's emails. Three CDs and three banker's boxes later, John had succeeded.

This story illustrates one consequence of the dramatic change between Grant's experience and Justin's. The act of communicating via letters has been almost entirely replaced by email or other types of electronic messages. Email has many incredible benefits and is certainly progressive, but as email is rarely printed to be saved physically, we must recognize that it radically changes the nature of the medium.

Physical to Digital

Just as soldiers have largely replaced letters with digital communications, we must realize that digital things are quickly replacing physical things in our lives. It's strange that the significance of the change is going mostly unnoticed. This is probably because we haven't invented new types of artifacts: We still have photos, videos, and letters. What we *have* done is transform the way we create, experience, share, and pass media on to future generations. This transformation has largely removed the physical objects from our lives and has left us with only the digital representations. We have yet to understand the ramifications of such a fundamental shift, and by the time we do, it may be too late to save the digital assets that are important to you and may one day become family heirlooms.

Look at the artifacts around your home or office (or in your computer or mobile device). Who's in them and what are they of? Chances are that they're of family and friends, some dear and departed. They probably show important events or capture moments from the past that remind you of what is important and why life is worth living. These objects become some of the most treasured items that we own and are often passed from generation to generation.

But the digital revolution is happening, and we are rapidly replacing many of the most meaningful types of physical objects in our lives with their digital counterparts. Photos, home videos, love letters, and stories from the front are all going digital. At the core of the shift is the separation of the physical object from the content that the object represents.

Photography is one of the most striking examples of the shift. For 130 years a photograph has been an image captured on a sheet of paper: a physical object that can be handed down to subsequent generations. The object, its meaning, and its value were intertwined—inseparable.

The shift to digital unravels this connection. Maybe we should pause, as we rush to embrace digital media, to consider if this is entirely a good thing, and to consider the ramifications of such a shift.

In only a handful of years, gelatin film photography has been swept away by digital photography. It's now nearly impossible to find good film cameras for sale (except in the specialty and used stores) and we all know why. Buying film, processing, and printing bad photos was the price people paid to capture that one great photo in a roll. Now the limitations and annoyances of the old medium are gone (and good riddance). But digital photography has changed more than the hardware that we use to capture images.

Different cameras over the years, getting smaller and more connected.
Photo by Britt Brown

It's now possible to shoot hundreds of photos to find that one that is right. The new pattern is to shoot many, cull them, and share them. At the same time we seem to have largely done away with the practice of printing and storing physical pictures. With the introduction of the personal computer, the Internet, and mobile devices, printing seems unnecessary because we can share and enjoy them in wondrous new ways: slideshows, email, Facebook, and Flickr. There are also digital photo frames sitting on desks and devices to send digital photos right to your living room television. But this lack of physical artifacts and our dependence on computers introduce new issues that need to be addressed, such as ownership, curation, storage, safety, and longevity. And death further complicates the issue. As a result the photos belonging to a departed loved one can be thrown into limbo or lost entirely.

The Benefits of Physical and Digital

Physical and digital objects have lots of things in common. Both need to be curated and cared for over time. Without a conscientious curator, both physical and digital objects would quickly vanish. Both give us joy, remind us of the past, and help us focus on what is important. But the way we interact with them is different because each has unique properties.

PHYSICAL OBJECTS	DIGITAL OBJECTS
May be fragile or may last for centuries	Are both fragile (easily deleted) and resilient (can be preserved forever if stored and curated properly)
Can be held as other people have held them. This physicality connects the current owner to previous owners	Are not tangible and have no physicality
Exist in only one place at a time	Can exist in an infinite number of devices and be copied endlessly. They are portable and can be sent and received easily over networks
Are clearly possessed by one person since each object is unique	Can be owned by many people
Are scarce or unique, which adds to their value	Can be easily duplicated, which may decrease their perceived value
Have survived through time and through events that we may want to connect with, if we know the stories	Can have metadata added to provide additional information that is not obvious
Take up physical space that makes managing huge quantities a daunting task	Require minimal physical space, but their quantity may be overwhelming
Break down over time and show their age	Won't break down or age; will look the same in the future as they do today
Need to be physically moved to be given or transferred to another person	Can be lost without proper access to them or become unreadable if the software to open them is no longer available.
Need care and proper storage to survive	Require electricity, computers, and software to read the file and display the data

Signs of the Changing Times

People often keep magazines or newspapers to commemorate important events. John bought newspapers and magazines on the newsstands when his son was born. At the time he wanted to capture the news from the day of his son's birth. He never thought that the very fact that the magazines and newspapers were physical would be as much a sign of the times as the news they contain.

What Do We Lose? What Do We Gain?

Physical objects can undoubtedly create a strong connection to the past since they were part of it. Each physical item has a story and a history of its own. Objects that have survived through time and been part of another person's life have a way of becoming precious and connecting with us in profound ways. As they break down, the patina that they gain becomes part of what makes them special. Letters on old paper, faded photos, and movies that are grainy and flicker all show their age. We lose these special qualities of physicality in the shift to digital. But we gain a lot too.

Digital objects can conquer quantity. Consider the change that we've seen in the way people store their music. Entire shelves full of CDs are now stored on an iPod that fits in the palm your hand.

Entire shelves of media can be condensed into one digital device.
Photo by Britt Brown

Digital objects can also drastically reduce the cost of creation. This lowered cost has enabled people to focus on quality. Now, instead of shooting one or two shots on the digital camera, you can instantly check and say, "Let's take one more. Mom blinked in that one." But a process of curation is needed with digital items too. We rate photos, star our important emails, and tag content that is important. Picasa, Google's photo editing and sharing solution, can automatically tag photos with the names of each person in the photo using face recognition.

Face Recognition

A friend added scanned photos of his father as a young man into his photo collection. Picasa's face recognition confused pictures of him and his father at the same age because they looked so similar.

Genetics 1, Google 0.

Digital tools also allow people to express themselves in constantly new ways. Photos can be brought into home movies. Desktops and screen savers can show the faces of the people we love. As computers and mobile devices evolve, they enable us to do new and fantastic things with our media: podcasting, making music, creating websites, sharing on social networks, putting together slideshows. The list goes on. It's fun to play, share, and explore digital media.

Judging from current trends, it seems that the world has decided that digital content creation is better. But, as a society, we have not thought through the ramifications or considered what will happen to all this digital content. Let's try to become more conscious of the effects that the digital lifestyle has on our own lives and legacy.

CHAPTER 3

A WELL-LIVED (DIGITAL) LIFE

" Advances in computer technology and the Internet have changed the way America works, learns, and communicates. The Internet has become an integral part of America's economic, political, and social life. "
—Bill Clinton, August 2000

Bill Clinton, love him or hate him, was right about the Internet. It *has* changed our economic, political, and social life. However, it's healthy to remember that the Internet is built on basic human experiences. We are still born, we live, and we die. Life itself has not changed, but the way we experience that life is changing radically. Technology and the Internet are fundamentally changing the *ways* that we communicate, create, learn, and work. And as we shall see, this technology is even changing how we experience death.

Ruth Osmun as a young woman.
Photo courtesy of Sue Romano

But let's go back for a moment. John's grandmother, Ruth Osmun, was born in 1917. She, like many in her hometown of Stanhope, New Jersey, probably called the "electric bill" the "light bill" since that was the primary household use of electricity. Technology was absent from her home until she got a phone and electric household appliances in the 1920s.

As a young mother, she had relegated the record player to the basement after her oldest daughter had played Fats Domino's "Blueberry Hill" too many times. Instead, Ruth preferred her radio. It was always on, playing radio shows, music, and news. Then in the early fifties, after all the neighbors had already gotten one, she and her husband finally bought a TV.

Her job as a legal secretary meant she lived behind a typewriter. These manual machines did not have an erase key—one error and you had to type the whole page again. Once she had mastered the machine she began to type everything. Letters, recipes, notes. To her, the electric typewriter was a powerful new invention that improved her life.

Consider for a moment that she never had a mobile phone or a digital camera. Banking always meant going to the bank and news always meant a newspaper, or radio and later television. She never sent an email, because she never saw the Internet. And she certainly never had a Facebook profile. To her, connecting with a friend was in person or in a typed letter.

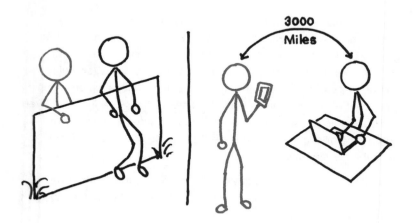

Two neighbors chatting beside their shared fence and two friends chatting 3,000 miles apart.

If we compare this to people today we see that technology has become an integral part of daily living. Let's take Evan, for example. Evan's iPhone is on him throughout the day, glows at his bedside each night, and waits to wake him in the morning. Before getting out of bed, Evan checks his email, calendar, and social networks. Those are his modes of communication and they help him plan his day. It's not surprising that they're his first stop daily.

In today's digital lifestyle technology is with us 24 hours a day.
Photo by Britt Brown

Evan uses his laptop and his mobile device to take photos, make phone calls, send email, schedule his day, listen to music, get directions, read or watch the news, pay his bills, learn new skills, connect with his friends, write articles, do his banking, watch TV, and play games. His car connects to his mobile device as does his entertainment center, which streams music and movies from the Internet. Even this book was written using Google Docs, an Internet-based word processing application. "Connected" might be an understatement for describing Evan's lifestyle.

Almost every aspect of his day is assisted or accomplished using technology, with the possible exception of the tortillas that he lovingly makes by hand (and *man*, he makes a mean taco).

As you can infer from Evan, and many others like him, the Internet is becoming an integral part of modern life. It's changing the way we interpret the world around us and experience our days. **The cumulative effects of this technological change are creating a seismic shift in our culture.**

> ### Internet or Web?
>
> What's the difference? People often use the names World Wide Web (the Web) and Internet interchangeably, but they are not quite the same. The Internet is a global data communications network that enables computers to connect to each other. The Web is a system of interconnected websites and pages. The Web is a system transmitted via the Internet.

Culture Shift

A seismic shift in our culture? What's causing that? How is it that in only a few years we have converted so many physical processes and objects to digital? As we look at the changing world we see many changes driving the shift. We're using different tools, we're more connected, and, perhaps as a result, today's generation is different.

Our Tools

We have desktop computers, laptops, smartphones, and tablet PCs. Their power is increasing and their physical size is decreasing yearly. Along with computers came a host of peripherals and imaging devices, such as digital cameras, digital video cameras, printers, and scanners, and the list goes on. Each device has transformed entire media ecosystems. And each one is running software that is improving almost daily, delivering greater functionality, features, and choice. Without a doubt the rapid development of technology is one of the core drivers of this cultural shift.

Perhaps the most significant development is the Internet. It's evolving at an incredible pace, and is transforming every industry and medium. It's connecting the world and fueling a generation of hyperconnected and informed people.

All these amazing new capabilities come with a price. Computing, while granting us amazing new powers over our content, has placed new requirements on us to keep current and constantly replace our tools—even when they still work. The relentless progression of technological innovation did not always move at such a fast pace. For centuries, people built tools to last. They fixed them when they broke and used them until they were worn out.

The technology recycle bin at the office is a treasure trove of outdated (i.e., five-year-old) technology.
Photo by Bruce DeBoer

But today we think of our technological tools as being largely disposable. Most people buying electronics know full well that they will be discarded before they break. Keeping them isn't an option since they are not built to last. And if they did last, they would become obsolete and useless. Most people replace mobile phones every year and a half. Consider yourself lucky if you get five years from your computer.

Connectedness

Laptops, tablets, and mobile devices are everywhere and they're connected to the Internet thanks to new mobile connectivity offerings and Wi-Fi hot spots that have popped up at every coffeehouse and café. People are now connected everywhere they go.

The ubiquitous presence of smartphones has been a particularly powerful driver of this new connectedness. It used to be that we pulled out the camera on special occasions to take a few shots. But today smartphones allow us to take photographs, email, text, capture video, and make phone calls (almost forgot that one) with a single device that fits in a pocket. They have enabled us to become prolific publishers, always creating new content and interacting with each other, even when we're hundreds of miles apart.

Generational Differences

Perhaps as a result of technology, but likely due to other factors as well, a generational change is also fueling the shift. The millennial generation is made up of people born between 1980 and 1999. According to the Pew Research Center this will be one of the largest and most well-educated generations in American history. This is also the generation that believes their use of technology is their defining characteristic. According to Pew, "Millennials have a distinctive reason for feeling distinctive. In response to an open-ended follow-up question, 24% say it's because of their use of technology." That's twice the percentage of Gen Xers, who are the only other generation to cite technology usage as a distinguishing trait.[1]

Generations Explained

It's easy to confuse the generations, so here's a quick reference by birth year.

Digital Natives 2000–present

Millennials 1980–1999

Gen X 1965–1979

Boomer 1946–1964

Silent 1926–1945

It's shocking that Gen X will be the last generation to remember a time before computers or mobile phones, and that within two generations the world will be populated with Digital Natives. **As the Millennials and Gen Xers age, people with a lifetime of digital assets will begin to plan for their death. If these cultural movements continue, preservation of digital assets will become as important as physical preservation.**

---

1. © 2010 Pew Research Center, Social & Demographic Trends project. "Millennials: Confident. Connected. Open to Change." http://pewsocialtrends.org/pubs/751/millennials-confident-connected-open-to-change.

Millennials outpace older Americans in technology use[2].

	MILLENNIAL (18–29)	GEN X (30–45)	BOOMER (46–64)	SILENT (65+)
Internet Behaviors	%	%	%	%
Created social networking profile	75	50	30	6
Wireless Internet away from home	62	48	35	11
Posted video of themselves online	20	6	2	1
Use Twitter	14	10	6	1
Cell phones and texting				
Used cell to text	88	77	51	9
Texted in the past 24 hours	80	63	35	4
Texted while driving	64	46	21	1
Have a cell phone with no landline	41	24	13	5
Median number of texts in past 24 hours	20	12	5	—

Note: Median number of texts based on those who texted in the past 24 hours.

Our Growing Dependence on Digital Institutions

As we move more of our media to digital formats and store more of our assets on the Internet, we will inevitably become more dependent on technology companies. These companies will provide network communications, personal connectivity, and online services that enable us to store and share our digital content. Because of this, connectivity to the Internet from computers and devices will become paramount. To be disconnected will mean a lack of access to your own important content.

---

2. © 2010 Pew Research Center, Social & Demographic Trends project. "Millennials: Confident. Connected. Open to Change." http://pewsocialtrends.org/pubs/751/millennials-confident-connected-open-to-change

Trust

Even if we have connectivity, we need to look at the huge amount of trust that we are placing in our online services. These private companies are often the sole home for our content. We depend on them and trust them more each year. We see this most clearly when one of these companies betrays our trust.

In April 2010, Facebook changed its privacy policy. Users saw this graphic:

The Facebook Instant Personalization alert.

Unless you clicked "Understand Your Privacy" you would not have known that "partner sites" suddenly had access to your personal information.

There was backlash from the community. A wave of status updates warned friends to opt out. A Google search for "Facebook instant personalization backlash" lists blog posts around the Web that called the alarm to change your privacy settings and to demand more privacy from Facebook.

The main problem was that Facebook did this as an opt-out enhancement, meaning that your data was shared, without your express permission, unless you actively opted out. It didn't help when a security hole at **www.yelp.com** enabled people to gain access to a Facebook user's name, email, and public data. In the end, this barely put a dent in Facebook's meteoric growth, but it did lose Facebook some trust and it made privacy concerns at their site a public issue.

Cultural Institutions

We have begun to think of these companies as if they are permanent, when in fact many are barely a decade old.

Snapfish, formed in 2000, is one of the oldest photo sharing services. Flickr, the largest, was formed in 2004. Often people upload their photos directly to these services from home computers and more frequently from mobile phones. As a result, these private companies often become the sole home for many people's photos.

Many Internet companies will fail or be bought up by larger companies. It's an odd phenomenon that people trust them so much. It's as if we think they are too big to fail. But this is not the case; they're often much less stable than we realize.

Consider the case of **Ma.gnolia.com**, a widely used social bookmarking service. In January 2009 they suffered a catastrophic database failure and their sites were taken offline. Much of their user data was lost and the service officially closed, after helping users recover as much of the lost data as they could. Several months later, they relaunched the service as a private offering called **Gnolia.com** and haven't gained the adoption levels that they once held.

Despite the data loss, the Ma.gnolia story is a best-case scenario of companies helping their users after a data loss. Let's consider the multimedia blogging service Utterz. Utterz allowed users to easily post images, video, and audio to their blogs. You could actually call a telephone number and record a post or send a photo via text message. Despite the fact that this information was later posted to your blog, the recordings and photos were hosted on the Utterz servers. Utterz was later renamed Utterli and its servers were shut down in April 2010 without warning. We know of several bloggers who lost content, but the full impact of Utterli's demise is unknown.

What's the lesson here? The Web is full of new companies and they're quickly creating communal places for their users. If these companies go out of business, or shut down their services, people will lose their content forever. These companies have a responsibility to millions of users and that's something that we must consider.

Each Individual Makes a Culture

Will the shift in technology and culture change our attitudes toward digital artifacts? If our tools aren't built to last and we are inundated with digital content, will people also begin to think of digital artifacts as being less important, or ephemeral?

This line of thinking leads to many questions:

- Will future generations have less attachment to physical objects since they haven't been part of their creation?
- Will people ultimately cease to care or stop having emotional attachment to physical objects?
- Should we encourage the creation of physical objects?
- Will future generations have a stronger attraction to digital things?
- If we don't keep our digital assets around long enough to care for them, will they begin to lose their meaning as well?

The answers to these questions will become clear only with time. For now we know from Pew Research that people across all generations believe that technology makes life easier, connects us, and makes us more efficient.

We should all ask ourselves a few questions: Is the shift to digital adding value to our lives? There are certainly times when the shift to digital communications and media is beneficial, but in the end what is the net worth?

We like to think that each person's individual answer has merit, but we humans are social creatures. We want to participate. A combination of new benefits and mass adoption is creating a massive amount of social pressure to make the switch. That pressure isn't waiting for us to think through the issues. We urge you to think though the decision and figure out how to preserve and pass on your assets in this new digital world.

CHAPTER 4

THE ARTIFACTS OF YOUR LIFE

You may not realize it but you're the exact cause of this cultural shift to digital things. You, along with millions of others, are creators and collectors, curating a rich collection of digital things around you.

It's easy to assume that your digital things aren't significant. After all, they take up virtually no physical space and you don't see them everyday. But as you live an increasingly digital life, this collection grows. It's more than just computer data, it's a set of artifacts that has the potential to chronicle your life.

Throughout this chapter, envision yourself at the center of a digital universe of content. We'll explore each part of it, how much you have, and where it's stored.

You're at the center of a rich collection of digital content.

Digital Creations

Within the universe of your digital things, you're most closely connected to the things that you create. People have created things for centuries, that's nothing new. Digital technology, however, has changed the way we create and the amount we create. You probably create new digital things everyday, but if asked to name all those things you probably couldn't. That's because we don't think twice about many of them.

You're creating new digital things, like photos, email, and videos.

If asked to think of the things you have created, you would probably list things you spent a lot of time and energy on. Maybe it's a song or the perfectly shot photograph. These works of art are certainly things you created and are important parts of your digital content, but there's much more than that to consider.

Do you think of your Facebook profile as your creation? How about your tweets (brief status updates posted on **twitter.com**)? These new means of expression are a part of the Internet called Web 2.0 or the Social Web. It includes websites that would not exist without the content that its users create. These sites actually encourage us to create content. Some reward us in some way for our contributions. Others rely on social pressure from our friends to participate.

Individually and cumulatively, the small things you create are an important part of your digital content. Small things like Facebook status updates, tweets, and blog comments should all be considered. You probably couldn't name all of these individually, but they are connected back to you via an identifier like an email address or user name.

Of course, you need to consider the more significant digital things you create, like photos, emails, and videos too. Not to mention those things that you may have converted from analog by recording or scanning them.

Digital Reflections

In most cases, your content is not created in isolation. It's connected to others within a content ecosystem.

You create something new when you reflect upon someone else's content. And it happens in reverse when they reflect upon your content. Either way, these contributions add up to something greater than the sum of its parts.

Aggregates

Let's say you create a blog where you post quotes, photos, and videos that you find interesting. The blog itself, as an aggregate, is a new expression even though the components were created by someone else. A friend of ours has created a blog at Tumblr (shown on page 35). The collection of entries on his tumblelog is uniquely shaped by his interests and expresses a new idea, one that's greater than the ideas that each original object expresses individually. Even if you do not have a blog, you're doing the same thing when you share a link on Facebook—perhaps to say you "like" this book. It's another way of saying that you identify with the content in question.

Shared Interactions

Increasingly, social websites allow us to respond to the content of others, and vice versa. The most classic example is a comment on a blog. After reading the post, you can add your own ideas at the end. Often this starts a conversation between two or more people. Your comment is clearly marked as yours, but it has a relationship back to the author of the article or to other comments. In this case, your comment is a new creation that reflects on their post and your attitudes.

You reflect upon the content of others and participate in shared interactions online.

Regardless of who starts the conversation, these interactions add to your own content and to theirs at the same time. Internet-based communication has given us the first reliable opportunity to document and study these shared interactions. It's helped us realize that you can learn a lot about a person from the way others respond to them. Fascinating stuff. Your participation is part of your collection. Your participation in these interactions is a creation of your own.

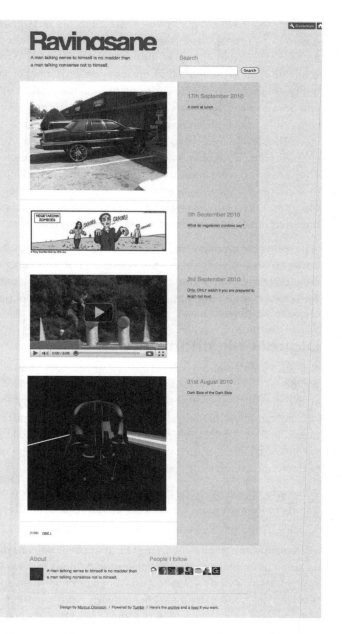

Ravingsane, a tumblelog curated by a friend of the authors (anonymous by request).

You should also know that these interactions are not generally as drawn-out a process as this analysis might suggest. It happens rapidly and almost without notice. Twitter is a great example. To many, Twitter is an information network. It's how they remain connected to the happenings among their friends and around the world. Let's say that you post a tweet that offers your opinion on a current event. Others who agree or disagree could decide to respond by expressing their view. Those who agree might retweet or post a copy of your message, sending your opinion out to their followers with their blessing. They are effectively aggregating your thoughts along with others into their profile. Or they might agree only in part and add their own new thoughts. Others might respond by creating new posts that disagree, but, in all cases, they have reflected on your original post.

New forms of communication continue to break down the separation between creation and reflection. These acts of communal content creation stretch our understanding of ownership. But regardless of who owns it, your contribution adds to your digital collection.

Digital Collection

It probably isn't your mission in life to amass a collection of things, but you do so whether you realize it or not. We tend to think of collections as groups of things that have a specific theme. You may know people who collect physical things like coins, teddy bears, or decorative plates. In those collections one thing holds true: The collection has a theme. And the collector can easily tell you if a particular object does or does not belong in the collection.

While you may have many collections, all the things you own combined create a greater personal collection where the theme is you. You are the arbiter of what belongs or does not belong.

Increasingly, the things you gather for that collection are digital. This includes both things that you obtained and things that were sent to you. Songs you've downloaded on iTunes or email messages you've received are good examples. These things were created by someone else, but you now have a copy of them in your digital collection and your copy is exactly like theirs. That's one of the most powerful ideas about digital files: Two can be exactly the same.

You gather new things for your collection all the time. We get this content from friends, colleges, and family.

So, there you have it: The things you gather join your greater digital collection alongside the new things and reflections you've created. That sounds like a lot of content, and that's exactly the case. And, you guessed it, it's only going to grow.

How Much Do I Have?

You have a lot of data—much more than you realize. But to help you understand the magnitude, we're going to put that statement into context. Let's first break down how digital assets are measured: You can count how many items there are, and you can see how much computer disk space they take up—their file size.

File Sizes

The more content you have in a computer file, the larger it is. I'm sure you've experienced file-size limits when trying to email large files. There is a range of file sizes (see the list below), but it makes more sense to talk about size in context of things you create, like documents, photos, and videos.

Let's say that you have an 8,000-page document. That's roughly the length of this book 40 times over. That may seem like a lot, but in terms of file size it's about 80 megabytes, without any images.

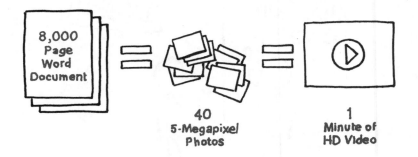

As a comparison, 80 megabytes is about the same file size as 40 5-megapixel photographs. You can fit roughly 325 of those on a CD.

Let's make one more comparison. The iPhone 4 creates HD video (720p) that will consume 1.3 megabytes every second. This means that a minute of video is the equivalent of 40 5-megapixel photos.

Units of File Storage

Here's a handy list to show the increments of file storage. It all starts with a bit (b), which is the smallest piece of data, stored as either 0 or 1.

Byte (B)	8 bits
Kilobyte (KB)	1,000 B
Megabyte (MB)	1,000 KB
Gigabyte (GB)	1,000 MB
Terabyte (TB)	1,000 GB
Petabyte (PB)	1,000 TB
Exabyte (EB)	1,000 PB
Zettabyte (ZB)	1,000 EB

Your Footprint

You're probably thinking, what do these files sizes have to do with my digital collection? As we said above, it's the unit of measure for computer file size. So let's figure out the potential size of your digital collection.

In 2008 Google reported that it was processing 20 petabytes of user-generated content each day. Stephen Bulfer, CEO and founder of **LifeCellar.com**, estimates that we'll each create 88 gigabytes in a lifetime.

As of this writing in 2010, there are 1.75 billion active Internet users worldwide. Based upon Google's assertion, Bulfer calculates that each user generates 3.3 megabytes daily. With a 75-year average lifespan, that's 88 gigabytes in a lifetime. That number contains only the things you create and share online—that estimate could still be low. Considering that the content we create grows more sophisticated daily and thus file sizes are soaring higher, we can only predict that the amount of content will continue to grow.

It's difficult to quantify exactly how much data we're talking about, but consider these facts: YouTube has reported that 24 hours of video are uploaded to their servers every minute. And the Radicati Group has projected that an average of 247 billion emails are sent per day. We could go on and on naming big numbers, but you get the idea—we're creating a lot of data.

Where Is It?

Today your content probably exists all over the place. Most, if not all, of it is located either on a computer or storage device in your home or office or on a server somewhere that is connected to the Internet. In computing, we refer to storage on your computer or device as *local storage* and storage on Internet servers as *cloud storage*. Over the past several years, especially since the emergence of tools like Facebook, Flickr, and YouTube, more and more content is stored in the cloud. Let's use your photos as an example.

Your content is transitioning from physical storage to local digital storage to cloud storage.

Until ten or fifteen years ago, a photograph was a physical product that was either developed at a lab or instant, like a Polaroid. If you wanted to store your photographs, you probably put them in a box or photo album in your home. When digital cameras emerged, suddenly we could have a digital photo instantly. The product was digital and had to be stored in a digital medium. Of course, you probably printed some digital photographs, but I bet you have many, many more stored on your computer than printed.

But we're not just keeping these photos locally on our computers; we're placing them on the Web for others to view. Websites like Flickr and Picasa specialize in helping us do just that. Now we even have smartphones that allow us to shoot and share a photo in seconds.

We're pushing content into the cloud and in effect scattering our photos across numerous computers on the Internet. While this may be more difficult to manage, the ability to access them from anywhere and easily share them with others is quite desirable.

This shift to cloud storage is significant and one of the primary reasons we wrote this book. One of many issues with preserving your digital content is that much of it does not reside on a computer over which you have direct control. Increasingly individuals are relying on websites to store their content, and that can cause numerous problems if the service goes out of business or the password is lost. We'll talk more about these challenges in Chapter 5, The Value of Digital Things, and in the second half of this book we will help you overcome them.

Who's Responsible for It?

In short, you are solely responsible for your own digital content. As we said earlier, you're at the center of it and it's through your curation that it's all connected. After you die, those connections may cease to exist and your collection of content can drift apart. With physical things, that's exactly how it happens. After an individual's death, the surviving family comes to the residence, divides up the possessions, and takes them as their own. Suddenly the original collection no longer exists.

You have a chance to change that. One of the unique features of digital things is that two exact copies can exist or one copy can be accessed in multiple places at one time. Your digital content can remain connected to you, but still be in the care of your heirs. It's a possibility that's quite exciting.

So What?

At this point you've considered your digital content, where it might be, how much you have, and your responsibility for it. And your next question is probably, "Why do I care?" That's a good question.

With many of our possessions in digital form and new assets continually being created, a significant and growing part of your estate is now digital. All of these digital things are more important than you might think. That's exactly what we're going to talk about next.

CHAPTER 5

THE VALUE OF DIGITAL THINGS

Let's face it: Death and digital legacy are not the easiest things to discuss at a cocktail party. We've been there. People often shrug off the conversation, and say they don't care about their digital legacy, because they'll be dead. So, why does it matter? Consider this: Why do you bother making and collecting digital things? If you don't care about them, why create them in the first place?

Maybe you believe that some things are truly ephemeral and that their value doesn't extend past their immediate use, like a quick message that you're running late. But we believe that most things you do online *are* valuable, even if you don't think so at the time. If you use Facebook, it's probably because you find keeping up with your friends valuable. It's not that it's financially valuable or that you even like Facebook itself, but the content it delivers, like personal news, photos, and messages, makes your life better.

Value

Value is an interesting concept. Our personal ideas of value are both contextual and temporal, changing as situations and time change. We believe that objects are valuable for myriad reasons: You might find an object aesthetically pleasing or maybe it's a helpful tool. It could even be an emotional reminder of another time and place. These various reasons are essentially different types of values. These include monetary value, utilitarian value, emotional value, and historical value, among others.

Simply put, value can only be assessed in a specific context and as that context changes so does the value. Let's pause for a moment and observe how the value of an object can change over time

Let's consider this photo of Evan's grandfather, Wilber. Outside of Evan's family there isn't a high demand for this photo. Even if it was considered valuable in terms of its antique nature, Evan's print is a scanned reproduction from 2008. So in terms of monetary value, the budget frame it resides in is probably worth more.

A framed photograph of Evan's grandfather, Wilber.

Photo by Britt Brown

Let's change the context a bit. Let's say that we ask Evan about its value. To him it's invaluable. First of all, the subject of the photo is his now-deceased grandfather. Just considering that, the emotional value is high. Moreover, it was taken some 65 years before Evan was born. It's the only photo Evan has of his grandfather from this time period. Its value to Evan is highly emotional and cannot be quantified in currency.

Now let's jump one hundred years into the future. No living person will remember Wilber and the photo's emotional value may have faded. But it may have historical value to a historian or anthropologist. He or she may learn something from the contents of the photo, or observe trends from thousands of similar photos and discover some new nugget of knowledge.

Throughout this example you could see the situation and the time changing, as did the value of the object. With the changing nature of value it's important to realize that the things you own today may one day be exponentially more valuable to someone else, be they family, friends, or even historians.

It's also important to note that the way a piece of content is created (either analog or digital) has no inherent effect on its value because the source of the value is in a person's connection to it—not in the way it was captured. That's good to know because chances are that in the future every photo taken *will* be digital.

For example, Evan's future grandchildren may value a photo of Evan that will most certainly be digital. Let's say that because of failed hard drives, lack of good backups, or any other data failure, it comes to be that this photo of Evan exists only on Facebook. And let's say that it was posted by someone who believes that their online presence, including Facebook, is unimportant. Suddenly a potentially valuable part of Evan's legacy is at risk.

When local copies no longer exist, valuable assets might exist only in the cloud.

New Forms of Expression

It's easy for us to say that a digital photo is valuable, because we already understand the value of physical photos. The same is true for things like email. Remember the emails of Justin Ellsworth, the solider killed in Iraq, and how they're very much like the letters that Grant Wilson sent from Vietnam. But it's harder to say that tweets or Facebook posts are just as valuable, because they're new and we don't have a point of comparison.

We believe that new forms of expression like tweets and Facebook posts are indeed important to your legacy. As we live our lives digitally, these new forms of expression become a constant stream of information. You may now take quick snapshots of interesting things on your phone and post them to Facebook. Maybe you tweet about your dinner or who you're spending time with. You might check in at a place using something like Foursquare, Gowalla, or Facebook Places. You might even write blog articles periodically. This type of information, seemingly insignificant, is actually a lifestream that has the potential to reveal all sorts of information about you.

Cumulatively, the elements of your lifestream form something that sociologists call a projection of your identity. Your identity is essentially your inner self that's expressed in everything that you do. Each of us has a personal identity that's different from that of everyone else who ever lived. It's what makes you uniquely you, dictating your self-image, self-esteem, and individuality.

Lifelogging

Some individuals have committed themselves to lifelogging: creating a record of their entire lives. Armed with wearable computers with cameras, they record exactly what they see. Some simply take photographs at specific intervals; others create audio and video recordings of every second. It makes tweeting every ten minutes seem a bit more acceptable, doesn't it?

Before these new forms of expression, you probably didn't choose to write a note about your dinner or your coffee break. The time to create and share that note wasn't worth the value you'd receive. But now that it takes much less time to create, many people create an increasing amount of information like this.

An example of the new motivation to share ephemeral events online, here's Evan's latte from November 23, 2009.

Identity

A book about digital culture wouldn't be complete without a word about personal identity. When Shakespeare wrote, "All the world's a stage" in *As You Like It*, he was actually well before his time in explaining our modern interpretation of identity. In the late 1950s, Erving Goffman described identity as a dramatic performance in his landmark work, *The Presentation of Self in Everyday Life*. Goffman believed that individuals essentially perform for others as they project their identities. We won't go into the complexities of Goffman's analogy, but let's consider the idea that everything we do is a performance of our identity.

As we create this lifestream of information, we're actually projecting our identity into cyberspace, the new global village, just as Goffman envisioned us projecting to those around us. The primary difference is that our projections into cyberspace are, by their very nature, recorded and can be reviewed later. This is unlike in-person communications, where interactions aren't recorded automatically, as that would require special effort and equipment.

Identity projection is like an act on a stage, where the stage is the Internet, and the audience can be anywhere.

Faceted Identities

Goffman also believed that we project differently (that is, we behave differently or share different things) depending on the audience. In fact we see whole social networks devoted to specific audiences and specific types of interactions. For example, LinkedIn is a site dedicated to professional networking.

This fracturing of identity is necessary if we want to control the way we communicate to different audiences. It helps focus the online conversation on what is relevant and valuable. Your colleagues may not care what you are doing for the weekend, your family may not care that you joined a specific professional group, and your friends may not care that your aunt has bunions.

Facebook, the largest social network, has added functionality to allow you to facet your online communications. It has added the ability to create and manage Lists of people. You could, for example, create a list called "family" and restrict access to posts about your aunt's bunions to that group only.

The Edit Friends screen on Facebook.

It's interesting to observe that online interaction is starting to force us to be aware of our faceted identities. We've heard countless stories of individuals fired for what they have said on Facebook and, without a doubt, those communications weren't directed at colleagues, but rather at personal friends.

A Way to Save Face

There is growing pressure to accept "friend requests" from co-workers and family members on social networking websites. While we can think of a fistful of reasons that accepting is a bad idea, there are times when you may feel obliged to. If you are worried that you may offend or put off some of these people, create a list called "offendable" and add your sensitive family and co-workers to it. Then share with them only the posts that you know won't offend them.

Shared Experiences

This is where digital communications get interesting. We just said that everything you do is a projection of your identity, and your online communications are no different. In many online networks, the conversation isn't restricted to one person and in many cases you're sharing with a much larger group. As such, these new forms of expression become a platform for shared experiences. With every comment, Facebook Like, retweet, or any other form of response, others are reflecting on your identity.

Through shared online experiences others can reflect upon your identity.

By recording this shared experience, a very interesting collection of data is created. From a sociological perspective, this data not only reveals information about you, it reveals information about how others perceive you. In some way, that's related to their identities as well. While this type of information may seem ephemeral, many platforms actually keep a record of it.

So, Why Does This Matter?

After you pass away, the everyday things in your life will become significant to your friends and family. No matter how simple, your digital content is no exception; in many respects, it may become even more valuable. As the trends look now, the amount of digital information we create and collect is only going to grow. It holds the opportunity to preserve a rich picture of your identity—that's unprecedented at this point in history.

But above all, we remember the past by looking to the things of the past. Our digital things today, however novel they may seem, are tomorrow's things of the past.

CHAPTER 6

WHAT YOU LEAVE BEHIND

We are becoming a digital culture, with digital assets. Before we go much further we need to answer the question:

" **What happens to your digital stuff after you die?** "

This is the central question that we strive to answer with this book. As it stands right now, with a little preparation, your data can live on for the next generation and possibly much longer. But the purpose and form of your data's afterlife is still very much in flux.

A digital society must have a process to deal with digital assets after death just as our current society has a process to deal with physical assets. The pressure to answer this question will grow with each passing year. It will become imperative as younger generations, who fully participate in the digital lifestyle and have rich collections of digital content, begin to recognize their mortality.

Passing On Physical Objects

To understand our current digital dilemma, let's explore how a person's physical assets are handled after death.

People tend to begin planning for death as they become more aware of the finite nature of their lives. This tends to be around middle age, but disease or the death of a loved one can highlight the issue sooner. The birth of children may also prompt parents to plan for their untimely end in an effort to protect their children.

But regardless of the reason, when we prepare for our death we put plans in place to transfer our valuable objects (especially financially valuable assets) to other people. The transfer of these assets can be so contentious that almost every society has developed a process—codified into law and sometimes religion—to make sure that this happens in an orderly fashion.

This process varies from country to country. Many societies have *forced heirship* that requires certain assets be distributed certain ways. Others have more open models that allow a person to distribute assets according to his or her own wishes. In either case survivors first look to a legal will. In the absence of a will, they look to a set of legal, cultural, or religious conventions for direction. The heirs, often led by an executor, divide the physical assets and resolve the affairs of the deceased.

Passing on physical objects is straightforward. There's only one object in one place.

The cultural and legal tradition of ownership allows an individual to keep valuable objects and imbue them with meaning throughout his or her life. In some cases, they make plans ahead of time, handing off objects before they die, along with a story in an effort to preserve the object and its meaning. At death the bond between a person and their possessions is broken, and all the assets are either handed down, given away, or thrown away. Their context lost, the assets become the property of new owners. The meaning, sometimes lost, is almost always changed in the transfer.

Passing On Digital Objects

There are some fascinating possibilities for the long-term future of our digital creations. So let's start at the moment of passing. We know that the moment of physical death is not the end of a person's digital life. We already see people's digital assets living on in many ways. Profiles on social networks continue to be active. Email addresses continue to accept mail. Online services continue to operate (if someone pays the bill). For the time being, everything goes on like nothing has happened. In fact this continuity is often disturbing to survivors. When Facebook asks people to reconnect with someone who is deceased, it can be an unwelcome reminder of a lost friend or loved one.

Electronic Death Notifications

It's important to note that this situation, where the online service providers don't know of your death, is likely to change in the near future. Once death records are made available online, the Web will be "aware" of a person's passing. Online service providers will be able to automatically close, memorialize, or terminate services. But for the time being, nothing happens.

But without someone there to curate, or at least archive, your digital content, it will tend to fall into disarray and be lost. Or it may even be deliberately deleted.

Passing on digital objects often involves local or cloud storage and its inherent complexities.

Leslie Harpold started experimenting with blogging in the late 1990s. She created several websites, including www.smug.com and www.harpold.com, where she posted essays, blog posts, and photos. But she wasn't alone. She befriended a group of like-minded people who also posted autobiographical content on the Web. From these connections, a small community grew.

Unfortunately, Leslie Harpold died in 2006 at age 40. Since then, all of her writings on her personal sites, including all her beautiful essays, have been lost. According to several blogs, many of her online friends have attempted to republish her work, but her family has chosen not to allow them to do so.

Leslie's friends miss her writing because her work held personal value for them. They feel that her writing was part of their community and represents some of the early pioneering examples of the blog format. Now, regardless of what Leslie might have hoped to happen, her contribution to the early Web is lost.

Why Does This Happen?

Simply put, we don't consider digital assets when making estate plans or when thinking about our property. As such our cultural and legal mechanisms for passing along assets haven't changed to include digital assets. Most bloggers probably never consider what should happen to their blogs after their passing. In Leslie Harpold's case, in the absence of any record of her wishes, her digital assets now belong to her family, who have the legal right to do what they wish with them. As Rogers Cadenhead stated in a blog post in January 2010,

> Perhaps this is the way it should be. No one has found an email or web page where Leslie stipulated her desires for her work in the event of her death, leaving the decision to her heirs. But everything I learned about Leslie over the years tells me that she'd want this part of her to survive.

Without Leslie's documented wishes, there's nothing her online followers and fellow bloggers can do, regardless of how valuable her work may be to them. This example simply underscores the point that you should make known your wishes for your digital assets, to avoid a situation where there is ambiguity about your intentions.

The Boomers and Gen Xers have begun to face this issue as people in their generations, like Harpold, have begun to die. But as we discussed in Chapter 3, A Well-Lived (Digital) Life, these generations don't have nearly the level of technical adoption of the Millennial generation, who have not yet experienced significant numbers of deaths. This challenge will only grow with time. Imagine the amount of digital content that Digital Natives, the generation born since 2000, will create over their lifetimes.

So the question is not, "Will our digital assets outlive us?" because they most certainly will, at least for a little while. Instead, the question is, "Should we take steps to secure them so they can be preserved?"

If we choose to do nothing, there is a risk. As John describes it:

> **Should we do nothing, we're allowing our digital assets to be slowly lost, closed down, deleted, and removed—a sort of virtual decomposition, until there is nothing left except some scattered fragments that are untraceable to their original source.**

Why We Pass Things On

Judging from the amount of time and effort people put into wills and estate planning, it's safe to assume that passing on assets is an important activity for most of us. In the physical world we have tangible objects. We keep these objects and imbue them with meaning. For many reasons, they become valuable monetarily, historically, or emotionally.

The reason people want to preserve assets can be multifaceted. Let's take a moment and consider why people plan for death and see if there is a digital equivalent.

To Transfer Financially Valuable Assets

Transfer of wealth is a way to ensure the continuation and success of progeny and loved ones.

As part of this transfer, people bestow money, real estate, and objects of value on their heirs. Making sure that these financial assets are transferred properly is often of paramount importance.

Here we find a direct equivalent in the digital world. Websites can generate revenue via advertising, affiliate programs, and the sale of goods or services. Software can be sold. Networks have value.

More significantly, all of our financial recordkeeping and management is going online. Financial accounts such as banking, retirement, and insurance really weren't physical in the first place. But as people move to Internet-based control of their finances, these assets are quickly becoming digital entities.

The transfer and control of these assets will need to become a standard part of estate planning, since in the future many accounts will be managed entirely online.

To Transfer Objects of Family or Historical Significance

People gather or have been given objects that contain familial or historical significance. These objects usually connect the owner with extended family or forebears. They are often older objects, considered to be family heirlooms.

Any physical item can fall into this category. Clocks, jewelry, photos, family movies, furniture, and art can all be part of a familial legacy. Digital assets will certainly add to this list.

Many digital assets will inevitably become heirlooms. Home movies and photos have already gone digital. (When was the last time you captured a family event with a film camera or 8 mm movie camera?) Email between family members can capture important conversations such as correspondence with those in the military overseas. Genealogical accounts can contain valuable research.

Even though they may take time to develop family or historical significance, digital assets are already gaining value. And in a future where many tangible assets have been replaced by their digital counterparts, digital family heirlooms will become even more prevalent.

To Transfer Emotional Value

The current process for transferring physical assets from one generation to the next is great at making sure the financially valuable assets are passed on but isn't terribly good at transferring the emotional value of an object. This is because emotional value is harder to quantify and items that have this kind of value are often not part of a legal will. There is also often a difference between the value to the owner and the value to the inheritor.

Objects with emotional significance are by far the most likely to lose their value or change in terms of how they are valued. There are times when these objects aren't valued at all by heirs. Sometimes the opposite is true and mundane objects take on greater meaning.

For example, when John's grandfather passed away in 2001, he left a house and financial assets that were divided up according to his will. But he also left behind a pepper mill that had been on the family table since the early 1960s. His grandfather probably thought of it simply as the pepper mill, providing nothing more than the utility of grinding pepper. But all three children attached special emotional value to it. It was unique, and it was something that their grandfather had used every day for forty years. (Not to mention that it grinds peppercorns into the perfect consistency.)

But none of the siblings could decide who would get it since it wasn't listed in the will. So now the three siblings take turns. They each get it for a year, after which they wrap it up and hand it off to the next sibling in turn.

Value Changes from Person to Person

Why does an object's value change from person to person? Owners imbue objects with meaning that may be known only to that owner. Once the owner dies, these objects become part of a person's legacy. But death destroys the memories associated with the object and much of the meaning may be lost. Secondhand stores are filled with objects that are bereft of their meaning. In many respects, they're failed heirlooms.

The emotional value we ascribe to digital assets falls prey to the same problems as their physical counterparts. The meaning of the object is still separate from the object. It's true that metadata (hidden data that exists as part of a file that describes an object) may help resolve this issue. For instance, when managing photos, you could add metadata to the image file that would contain information like the date, description, photographer, and the people in the photo. But the addition of metadata can't solve every problem, and it requires a lot of work on the part of the creator.

It's sad but true: Some of our most treasured possessions are tomorrow's trash.

As we've seen, there are many reasons to pass on your objects, and there are digital equivalents of all these reasons. Digital objects may suffer from the same shortcomings as their physical counterparts.

But what would it look like if objects with financial, historical, and emotional value were not just passed down but preserved? What does it all add up to? There's a possibility that it could look like nothing we've ever seen before.

CHAPTER 7

THE OPPORTUNITY
OF DIGITAL LEGACY

Creating and leaving behind things for future generations can be a way to preserve a person's identity. The desire for immortality, or at least remembrance, is a persistent human trait. To see a master of immortality at work, look no further than Pharaoh Khufu or Emperor Qin Shi Huang. Over 4,500 years ago, Khufu built the Great Pyramid of Giza in order to leave behind the most spectacular tomb in history. And 2,300 years later, the first emperor of China's Qin Dynasty, Qin Shi Huang, took his shot at immortality when he commissioned the largest tomb ever built and a terracotta army—an array of over 8,000 unique clay soldiers and chariots that he would be able to command after his death. These were huge endeavors to show the world how important they were and to ensure that the world would never forget them. Their plans seem to be working marvelously.

Of course when we see these marvels we have to understand that these great men built them on the backs of their workers. Khufu spent hundreds of millions of manhours constructing his monument. Qin Shi Huang employed hundreds of thousand of men. These anonymous workers died with little or no fanfare and are forgotten as individuals.

Pharaoh Khufu's Great Pyramid.

Photo by Jérôme Bon

Qin Shi Huang's Terracotta Army.
Photo by Anita Ritenour

Now, most people don't get to build a 450-foot-high monument, mostly because they don't have hundreds of thousands of minions at their command. For the rest of us, a modest headstone or nameplate is the extent of our monument. But, make no mistake. These are identity objects just the same, meant to provide a meaningful, long-lasting memorial to one's life.

Wilber Hewett, Evan's grandfather, has a headstone that provides rudimentary information: his name, the dates of his birth and death, his spouse's and children's names, and his army service. He is buried in a sealed vault, in a sealed casket that contains a sealed tube with similar information in case the casket has to be moved.

While incredibly meaningful to the people who knew Wilber, his grave is one of many in the cemetery. Grave markers tend to look alike, and visitors get only the most basic information about the person buried there. But monuments are just one of many ways that we use to preserve our identities. If we want to be remembered as more than a stone in a field, we should consider taking a page out of Qin Shi Huang's playbook and take an active role in shaping our legacies *before* we die.

Wilber Hewett's final resting place in Shallotte, North Carolina.

Photo by Evan Carroll

This broader approach enables us to leave behind a more personal legacy. The general process most people use is to accentuate aspects of our personal history that we think are admirable and commendable, and downplay or ignore what we don't want remembered. We then collect and create meaningful objects that we pass on along as a way to reinforce that legacy.

There are many ways to do this:

1. Transfer your treasured possessions, along with their stories and meaning, to your heirs.

2. Write your memoirs to tell your story the way you want it remembered. Granted, a memoir can totally whitewash undesirable aspects of your life.

3. Create an ethical will to preserve your identity. The idea of this document, although not legally binding, is to communicate to your heirs your ethical and spiritual values, life lessons, and family history.

But even with these efforts, in the past it has been true that the deceased's identity inevitably became scattered. Without you there, your identity will slowly dissolve. Each asset becomes part of each heir's identity. In this way, your content makes it to the next generation and if it has meaning and value to the recipient, it stands a chance of being passed along into the future.

As you can imagine, identity preservation has a digital equivalent as well. Here we use digital objects in the same way we use physical objects. We attach stories and meaning to objects and pass them on. We can write memoirs and ethical wills as digital documents and pass them on. We can also add new types of content such as archives of our social accounts and conversations.

But in the new medium of digital communication, there is a greater opportunity to preserve identity—something that has heretofore been available only to kings, pharaohs, and emperors.

The Birth of the Digital Legacy

Your data is going to outlive you. The question is in what form and for how long.

In its simplest form, a digital legacy is a summation of the digital assets you leave behind for others. As the shift to digital continues, the digital assets left behind will become a greater part of your overall legacy.

These assets, to one degree or another, can be distributed in much the same way that physical assets are, meaning each one can be bequeathed to one or many heirs.

Assigning digital assets in this way is an important step because, as we have seen, most people aren't even doing this now. But if that's all we do, we've only dealt with our digital assets in the same way that we've dealt with our physical ones. At that point all we have is a digital equivalent of the physical world.

If your digital assets, like your physical assets, are simply passed on, they get incorporated into an heir's identity. This process still relies on another person to value them, take care of them, and pass them on in turn. But let's be honest about the effectiveness of this method: People may manage to get their digital assets passed to their children or loved ones, but this is no guarantee that those assets will live any farther into the future. The things you value may simply not be valuable to your heirs.

This brings us to a more arresting idea: Your digital identity could have a different fate. Maybe the identity you create over your lifetime can maintain cohesion after your death. Maybe the connection between the creator and creations (complete with the original meaning) can be preserved, maintaining the gestalt. In other words, your digital identity may have the opportunity to become a lasting, maybe even immortal, digital legacy—an expression and reflection of you that will survive far into the future.

This possibility represents an opportunity that has never before existed for ordinary people. Imagine a way that your intentions, accomplishments, values, and actions could be preserved for all time. You may not be as famous at Khufu or Qin Shi Huang, but your legacy could be just as accessible.

But How Could This Work?

There are many possible solutions, but the basic idea is to replace the live person curating an online identity with some kind of permanent digital record. This record would allow all the disparate assets on the Internet to point back to a source that would maintain your identity after your death.

There could even be connections back to real world memorials. We've already seen digital headstones for sale that have a chip that allows users to access information about the deceased on the Web. The result would be a richer physical and digital experience of the deceased.

Immortal Issues

It's true that we don't yet have a framework to maintain a cohesive posthumous identity. There are many other aspects to consider before we can truly suggest a permanent digital legacy.

Identification

The fact is we still don't have a unified way to manage and verify people on the Internet. But as the Internet evolves, solidifying an identity is becoming important. In 2007, the OpenID Foundation launched an effort to solidify identity on the Web. Then, in June 2010, the U.S government drafted the National Strategy for Trusted Identities in Cyberspace (NSTIC) to "develop a comprehensive Identity Ecosystem Framework."

One problem with most of the identity work so far is that it fails to consider the effects of death on identity. But this is something that many people (including the authors of this book) are looking to rectify.

Active or Passive Collection

There are two views of what a digital legacy is made of. The first is an active, managed legacy that contains only what the person wants as a part of it. It's human nature to want to forget the bad and mundane things and concentrate on the good and noteworthy. It's true that this kind of whitewashing may be disingenuous to one degree or another, but no more so than a photo album that only shows the good times. This kind of legacy might be appropriate for relatives and friends who want to reminisce or for a child to get to know a grandparent who died before his or her birth.

The other is a passive view of legacy, which would include *everything* you do online—every comment, email, tweet, video, and post. Everything added up equals your legacy. While this may be more accurate, it doesn't take into account importance or focus. Every piece of data is equal to the next. While the possibilities of a massive data store are intriguing, this could be overwhelming to a person in a raw form since it is a lot more data than you might think. Thankfully computers don't mind data quantity, and parsing the data could provide unique insights into a person's life.

Data Myning

But the reality is that all these assets are far more disconnected than you may think. There is currently no definite way to pull them all together. Think for a moment about how many people share your name. We have a friend named Paul Smith. Do you have any idea how many Paul Smiths there are? Well, a lot. Disambiguation is harder than you think. The Sociable Media Group at MIT's Media Lab recently created a project called Personas to demonstrate just that. They ask individuals to put their name into an interactive exhibit and it returns with a view of how the Internet sees you. If you ask it to process Paul Smith, you'll find a rather generic profile, as it chronicles all of the Paul Smiths in the world, not just our dear friend.

A new trend is "data myning," a term coined by **TrendWatching.com**, in which a person points to assets on the Web and says "this is mine, and this is not mine." The OpenID provider called ClaimID allows you to do just this. Perhaps it will help Paul Smith disambiguate himself from the fashion designer; the hotelier and namesake of Paul Smith's College; and countless others.

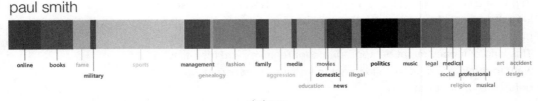

Personas result for Paul Smith. As you can see, he's quite the Renaissance man.

A ClaimID profile.

The Burden of Data and Emotional Economics

One thing to consider as you begin to think about your digital legacy is the fact that your digital content may be a burden to your heirs. You may have an overwhelming amount of data by the end of your life. You may have assets that are too messy and unorganized. You may have a lot of data that your heirs just don't really care about. It's sad but often true.

Consider a situation in which a photo collection is handed down from a parent to a child. The parent may want the child to have some photos to remember him or her by. The child may want photos from this parent's collection to remember his parent by. But it does no one any good to lob 10,000 photos at the child. The reality is that a behemoth collection will not be valuable to him or her. The photos might be kept out of a sense of guilt. But with all those photos, the chances of the child actually connecting with an individual photo is lessened because he or she would have to wade through 10,000 to get at the one.

This is a concept that we like to call emotional economics. The laws of supply and demand apply to emotional value just as they apply to markets. When supply is high, demand is low. If John has 10,000 photos of his beloved grandfather, chances are that none of them will be highly valued. There are just too many. It's the same feeling you get when your neighbors show you 300 photos from their vacation. By the end you just don't care anymore.

Do your heirs a favor and think ahead during your life and tend to your data. Curate and weed your collections. Consider tagging your favorites, deleting the duplicates, editing them, and tagging them. Got fifty of your birthday? Narrow it to five or fewer. You could certainly keep all of your photos, but be sure that your favorites are kept separately. Not only will this make inheriting those photos better, but it will make your life better as well, because chances are you will connect with those remaining photos in a much deeper way when there are fewer of them.

We hope this gives you an understanding of the possibilities that await us in the future. But before we marvel at our technological beauty and start planning our immortal legacy, we need to understand a sobering fact: All the digital content you have on the Internet is at risk, and if you don't do something about it, your content may be lost, left behind, or simply deleted.

CHAPTER 8

YOUR LEGACY AT RISK

Earlier in the book we introduced you to Leslie Harpold. Another early blogger was Brad Graham, who coined the phrase *blogosphere*. Both were hyperconnected pioneer bloggers who passed away unexpectedly. Yet today, Brad's sites are still online and accessible to the world. Leslie's however are not. Neither of them, to our knowledge, created a plan for their digital assets and both were very technically savvy, as were their friends. After their respective departures, their friends stepped in to help. They wanted to preserve these early blogs in the memory of their creators. So why the difference?

**Brad's website,
www.bradlands.com.**

In Leslie's case, her sites were removed from the Internet. In Brad's case, his hosting provider was kind enough to allow his friend, Matt Haughey, to take over the payments. In the absence of guidance from the deceased, it's hard to decide what should happen. **At this point in our growing understanding of digital legacy, the risk is high that your assets will be handled contrary to your wishes. To ensure that doesn't happen, you need to address these risks.**

Awareness

We've discussed how digital things don't take up much physical space and are transitioning from local to cloud storage. With this lack of physical presence, additional effort is required to ensure that your heirs know about your digital content. Some things like websites and social media profiles were designed to be shared. Chances are that your heirs will know about those things. But things like a blog written under a pseudonym or a character within an anonymous virtual environment are assets that your heirs may have no clue about. It's nearly impossible for your heirs to deal with something if they don't know it exists. With that in mind, the first barrier to overcome is awareness.

Without help, your heirs might not know about your digital content.

Identification on the Web

At present there is no programmatic way to disambiguate one person from another on the Web. Unless you have a unique name, a Web search for your name will return results related to multiple people. Services like ClaimID can help with this manually, but if we're to create automatic processes to collect and potentially archive a person's online footprint, we need better tools.

Consider the story of Justin Ellsworth. His father was aware of his email account. In fact, they had discussed creating a scrapbook of his messages once he returned home. In this case Justin's intentions were clear, but another barrier stood in his father's way: access.

Access

No matter what your wishes are for your digital content, access is an important issue to resolve. Even in the laws surrounding real property, access is considered. If your property isn't accessible without crossing another tract, you probably have an easement, a legal right to create an access road through a specified part of your neighbor's property. We need something similar in the digital world. Many companies on the Internet offer great services that can help you manage, store, and share your digital things. With each of them you submit to the company's *terms of service*. Many of these terms do not specify what will happen upon your death, and worse, some say that your account is *nontransferable*. That's legalese for "you can't give it to someone else."

Access information, like user names and passwords, is often necessary to build on, delete, or even leave digital things alone. In Brad Graham's case, Matt was probably permitted to pay for the hosting because of his relationship with the hosting company. His intentions were to never change the sites, but one of Brad's web forms was eventually overwhelmed with spam. The hosting provider then granted him access to clean things up.

Without access your heirs won't be able to carry out your wishes.

The chances that your heirs will gain access to carry out your wishes are unknown. It's important to resolve access issues before you pass away, because it can be a real nightmare later.

Control

Even with the central issue of access solved, it's worth considering who is actually in control of your digital assets. You're definitely the right person to specify what should happen to your assets, but who's going to carry out your wishes? The most logical solution is to appoint a digital executor to handle your digital affairs.

Digital Executor

A digital executor is a person appointed to handle the distribution of your digital assets after you pass away. We'll talk more about digital executors in Chapter 10, Before You Begin.

Even though Brad Graham didn't ask him to take on these duties, Matt fulfilled the role of digital executor in many respects. But unlike the executor of your estate, a digital executor is not legally obligated to carry out your wishes or authorized to act on your behalf. For now you can hand over access and hope that nothing else will stand in the way of your digital executor, but that might become harder in the future. There's an opportunity here to build an executor for digital assets into the estate planning process.

Ownership

As the creator of digital information, you have certain rights to what you created. Even though the asset is not tangible, it should be protected under intellectual property laws. But depending on what you do with that content, you may share those rights or give up some or all of them. Each time you register for an online service you agree to their *terms of service*, which basically state what the service expects of you and what you can expect in return. Services require these agreements to ensure that they're legally protected. Let's go back to the Ellsworths.

When Justin signed up for his Yahoo email account, he agreed to its terms of service. The agreement stated:

> You agree that your Yahoo! account is non-transferable and any rights to your Yahoo! ID or contents within your account terminate upon your death. Upon receipt of a copy of a death certificate, your account may be terminated and all contents therein permanently deleted.

In this case, a Michigan probate court disagreed and ordered Yahoo to turn over the emails—but you can't count on a similar outcome. And you don't want your heirs to have to go to those lengths. Even though it's fairly clear that the emails were the property of Justin Ellsworth, his ability to access them was controlled by the terms of service. When he passed away, so did his right to access the account. But the resolve of his family paid off with the court ruling. Unfortunately, that's probably an exception to the norm.

Depending upon where your content is stored and the provider's terms of service, you may not own your content.

Before we can expect that companies will respect the wishes of the deceased, new legal frameworks are necessary to deal with these issues. At present there's too much room for uncertainty and that's not fair to you or your heirs.

Preservation

It would be nice to say that your digital content could be preserved forever, but that's not feasible at this point. In order for your data to remain in existence indefinitely, a new kind of curator is necessary.

Digital files are only as reliable as the physical disks on which they reside. In the world of digital archives, the mantra is that multiple copies keeps stuff safe. That's absolutely correct. Redundancy and backups are essential to maintain file integrity. It's not possible for you to put a few disks in a safe and assume that they'll be readable in the future. You'll need someone to become the caretaker of your data to ensure that multiple copies are maintained.

For digital things to last, steps must be taken to preserve them.

File Formats

You'll also need someone to convert files from older formats or ensure that the technology needed to read these old formats is preserved. Google's Vinton Cerf, creator of the TCP/IP protocol (the communications that run the Internet), has postulated that we need to deal with our "rotten bits" and ensure that the technology to read today's file formats is preserved. Consider that today we use JPEG as the standard format for images. In the future, that standard might change. And if JPEG-reading applications are no longer available, you'll need someone to convert the files to newer formats and ensure they're maintained over time.

The core challenge here isn't the technical ability to do these things, but rather the manpower needed to do it. We could become burdened by our ancestors' data and that prospect isn't very appealing.

Old Media

It's also worth noting that we presently have the early forms of recorded images and video to consider. Countless videocassettes, reels, slides, negatives, and prints are home to precious family memories. But their physical nature is degrading as they reach the end of their life cycle.

If you don't digitize your old media soon, it may be lost forever. Go raid your parent's closet. Get all those reels and cassettes out and digitize them now. It may be your last chance to convert them into digital formats so they'll have a chance of surviving in our new digital world.

Life span

Physical media has a life span. After its life span, it will break down. In old movies or photo negatives, this means that the pictures fade. VHS tapes get grainy and the sound drops. Cassette tapes lose their quality. Eventually, all you'll have is static.

There is no easy answer to the question, "How long will my old media last?" The numbers can vary *radically* depending on the quality of the media as well as how the media was created, stored, and used. Properly created and archived, some media can last decades. But most media isn't, so act now.

The hardware necessary to play old media has a life span too. Even if you do store the media properly, the players and hardware are being replaced. Film projectors that break are often not repaired. VCRs don't even sell at garage sales and the thrift stores have piles of them. Good luck finding an 8-track or Laserdisc player.

Solution

So what should you do? First, get everything off the old media. Digitize everything. Getting everything transferred to a single format can help you manage things more easily.

Don't make the same mistake twice. Digitizing old media like VHS and putting them only on new media like DVDs won't help you because in another ten years (or sooner) you'll be faced with the same situation as the DVDs break down.

For movies, convert them to DVD (so you can enjoy them) *and* keep the movies on your computer as an MOV, AVI, or MP4 file. In the case of photos, consider printing them (printed photos can last up to fifty years) and keeping the digital files (most likely JPGs) on your computer. This eliminates the hardware dependencies and makes managing them a software process.

Once all these files are on your hard drive, back them up like any other file. Don't have a backup schema? Get one. We've got a list of online backup services in Chapter 11, Computers and Devices. This will effectively keep the files in three places, and keeping things in multiple places increases the likelihood that they will be preserved.

Digital Dark Age

In addition to the half century of magnetic and film media, we also have a smorgasbord of old digital technology and files from old unsupported software to deal with. The old media and old tech create a body of content that is locked in dozens of obsolete formats. If we, as a society, continue to neglect the content made from the 1950s to the 2000s, we stand to create a digital dark age—a stretch of time that is lost because the content is beyond rescue.

This is a problem that even the most sophisticated archives must deal with. In 2007 it was reported that The National Archives of the United Kingdom held a ticking time bomb of digital information that might not be readable in the future, because of its varied and obsolete formats, but they were doing something about it. Ideally they would have the resources to convert their information, but with more than 580 terabytes of data, that would be a monumental task. Instead they struck a partnership with Microsoft to virtualize older operating systems and software applications to ensure that the older formats would remain readable in the future.

Is it possible that we won't have records from the early days of computing, because we failed to preserve data properly or, worse, failed to recognize its importance?

These are big questions that can't be answered today. But we think the immediate goal should be to pass your data to the next generation. Perhaps in that time computing power will advance enough to help your heirs deal with this data in a meaningful way. Hopefully this strategy will give us the greatest possible chance of preserving this period in history, if each of us does our part and handles our personal share of the content.

What's Worth Preserving?

The risk of a dark age brings up the question of volume. Should we save everything we can? Or should we identify the most meaningful content and limit our scope? It's clear that we're creating more than we ever have before. With the ability to store this information in very small places and the ease of creation, we have no reason to limit our creations. But should we decide what's worthy for preservation beforehand? Or should we save everything and hope that our successors can deal with it all? Maybe we should do both, show the depth of what we thought was most important and provide the breadth as well.

Ethics

It probably goes without saying that you want to be remembered in a certain way. It's the way you perceive yourself—a reflection of your true identity. How can you ensure that will happen? Should your digital legacy be a passive collection of your digital content or should you have a say in curating what's most important? You also have to consider how to maintain your content in the future. Is it ethical for a caretaker to remove things in the future, perhaps to make things more manageable or palatable to them? On the other hand, is it appropriate for someone to add to your legacy, perhaps by continuing to post updates to your blog or Twitter account? These social norms don't really exist today and it's something that society will need to figure out going forward.

But Wait, There's Hope

Amid all these risks and questions, there is some good news. A small amount of planning today can drastically increase the chances that you'll be remembered the way you want to be in leaving behind your digital heirlooms. We'll help you through that planning in the second half of the book.

Perhaps even more comforting, archivists, attorneys, entrepreneurs, and people like us are already working to resolve these issues. In the next chapter we'll look at this emerging industry, how it started, what's available now, and what's next.

CHAPTER 9

THE BIRTH OF AN INDUSTRY

March 1999. That was a decade after Tim Berners-Lee invented the World Wide Web and some five years before Thefacebook (really, that's what they called it then) took the college world by storm. It's also when Michael Krim boarded a London-bound flight from Los Angeles. Amid severe turbulence some seven miles above the Atlantic, his mind turned to the inevitable: death. After a safe landing he set to work. By September he had created FinalThoughts.com, giving the Web its first service to help people prepare their online presence for death. FinalThoughts.com allowed users to store messages to be delivered posthumously via email. It was new and made quite a stir in the media.

For whatever reason, Michael Krim was a bit too early to market. By 2003 mentions of the service had faded and *The Daily Telegraph* reported its demise. Since that time some two dozen services have emerged to help individuals prepare digital estate plans and posthumous email messages.

Fast forward to July 2008. Jeremy Toeman was on a flight and, as a new father, found himself considering how his family would manage should he meet his demise. He remembered the trouble he faced a year earlier trying to access the Hotmail account of his deceased grandmother. The lightbulb went off and he went on to create **LegacyLocker.com**, a new digital estate planning service. It was about this time that the digital afterlife industry seemed to go into full force. Jeremy's company quickly gained attention in the media and the issue of digital death seemed to enter the minds of many.

Maybe it was all that turbulence, but entrepreneurs are hard at work to help deal with the issues of digital death. Their work is opening up new opportunities to secure your digital legacy, bringing you tools to create digital estate plans, send emails after death, and create online memorials. But with the World Wide Web still in its early twenties, we can only imagine what services, protocols, and social standards will be in place in the next several years. Let's consider how these advances are moving toward the idea of a permanent digital legacy.*

---

*Throughout this chapter we'll reference different online services and explain how they work. We've made every effort to ensure these descriptions are correct at the time of publication, but they could change in the future.

Legacy Locker, a digital estate planning service.

Digital Estate Planning

A new class of online services, like **LegacyLocker.com**, has emerged to help you create what amounts to a digital estate plan. After creating an account you can input your user names, passwords, and wishes for each of your digital assets. You can also specify an heir for each, who will receive your information after your death is verified, usually with a death certificate. These services, which also include **Entrustet.com** and **DataInherit.com**, have tackled some of the fundamental challenges we discussed in the previous chapter. By serving as a repository for your passwords and a means to notify your heirs, they have ensured awareness of and access to your digital assets.

It's actually quite a chore to collect all your user names and passwords for your various digital assets and content. Today this effort can provide peace of mind that your digital things will be accessible to the next generation. That's a significant a step in the right direction, but there's an opportunity to do more.

Passwords Might Not Be Enough

Remember that a user name and password only grant your heirs access. They don't actually take steps to keep your content around. If a service shuts down, you might lose access to that content. You should consider a strategy where you also make an archive and place everything, or at least the most important things, in one place, in addition to its original home. Now it's in two places. Isn't that better than one?

Password lists and heirs are in many respects a workaround for the problem. Ideally services that host digital content would have an industry-standard or legally enforced way to deal with the death of their members. There's a significant opportunity to design death planning into these services. While it's not easy to talk about death, it would be useful if services like Google or Yahoo allowed you to specify an heir to your account, granting them access with the appropriate documentation, like a death certificate. Some services like Facebook and Twitter have documented policies for deceased users, but only after the fact. It requires your survivors to take action, instead of you specifying wishes in advance. But, it is a step in the right direction. We're hopeful that policies will evolve to address death proactively. This type of plan would prevent you from revealing your password to others and relieve you of the burden of maintaining an inventory of your passwords.

Even with the advancements in social network policies, there's still a good deal of uncertainty. At present we lack legal frameworks and policies to deal with digital assets properly. The law was written with the qualities of physical assets in mind but hasn't been updated or reinterpreted extensively to account for digital content. Despite small victories like that of the Ellsworths and their son's email, there hasn't been a landmark legal battle that brought digital assets of the deceased to the forefront. We know of several individuals and organizations who are involved with these issues and hope that their work will be the catalyst for legal advancements in the near future.

Posthumous Messaging

For every service that helps with digital estate planning, you'll find two or three that send email on your behalf—written by you in advance, obviously—after you pass away. We'll talk about the mechanics of them in the second half of the book. While these services could easily be used to share passwords and wishes, they present a unique opportunity to communicate with loved ones after you die. Of course, this was possible with written letters, videotapes, and all other forms of physical media. The key difference is that you don't have to depend on others for delivery anymore. An email can be delivered electronically without involving someone else to hand it off or put it in the mail.

GreatGoodbye is one of several posthumous email services.

These messaging services afford you new ways to continue conversations after your death. Perhaps you want to tell your family how much you loved them. Or maybe you want to get the last word in on an old dispute. You could even attach videos, photos, or other documents. The possibilities for these communications really are endless, as you have the opportunity to craft just the right message for each person or group on your list.

You could also use posthumous messaging to distribute your ethical will, a document that communicates your philosophy on life or your values. This type of continuing guidance can serve as a living legacy of sorts, where you can continue to influence your loved ones after your passing through a document they can revisit over time.

Online Memorials

Long before Final Thoughts was created, the Web was already being used for memorials to various individuals who had passed away, many before the Web even existed. It's interesting to consider that some individuals who never had a digital presence of their own were remembered in online memorials. Often created by friends and family, these memorials contained some photos, sentimental writing, and guestbooks where others could post their own memories and condolences.

Online memorials are particularly unique because they transcend place and time. For instance, you might attend a memorial service at an appointed time and place or visit a gravesite or other memorial. Online memorials allow you to visit whenever you like from anywhere.

We're currently seeing a new wave of online memorial sites like **Bcelebrated.com, Online-Legacy.com,** and **MyWonderfulLife.com** that allow you to create your online memorial before you pass away. Inspired by the success of participatory sites like Facebook and Twitter, this type of sites allows you to create an initial profile that others can extend that after your death. It's a way for you to shape your legacy and have a say in how you'll be remembered.

There are also impromptu memorials that come about after death. We've heard of countless profiles on Facebook and other social networks that have become places for friends to leave comments, memories, and public messages for the deceased.

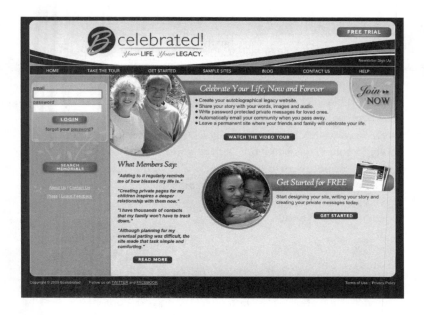

Bcelebrated, an online memorial site.

As entities that transcend place and time, online memorials have changed the bereavement process. Without a specific time or place for remembrance and shared consolation, we can engage in shared bereavement at any time. This allows individuals from different parts of your life to connect with each other, even if they hadn't connected previously, and perhaps honor your life in ways that were not previously possible.

This new form of memorial has interesting implications, especially in Eastern cultures that spend significant amounts of time honoring their ancestors. In China the annual Qingming Festival (Tomb Sweeping Day) generates record crowds year after year as the number of graves rises. To help alleviate the additional traffic and to solve issues with overcrowded cemetery space, officials in China are advocating the use of online memorials to honor the deceased through "virtual sweeping." In fact, Hong Kong started a government-funded boat service that allows families to spread the ashes of the deceased at sea. Hong Kong has set up an online memorial site as well to afford families a memorial for sweeping and remembrance while ashes are stored in homes or scattered at sea.

Other Services

Our digital lifestyles have also triggered the creation of several other companies that don't fit neatly into the categories above but provide unique value worth discussing here. Throughout the book we've discussed planning extensively in an effort to motivate you to secure your own digital legacy. The fact remains, however, that many have passed away without securing theirs. One service, founded in 2010, seeks to help in this situation. **DigitalEstateServices.com** offers survivors the opportunity to get into locked computers, archive the contents, and potentially discover user names and passwords for other services. This new "digital locksmith" helps you deal with the unkempt digital remains of another.

Backup Services

They're not really new, but if you don't know about online backup services, you should look into one. Having your content in more than one place helps keep it safe. And keeping it online can prevent a complete loss in case your hard drive fails, your computer is stolen, or your house is destroyed. These accounts are affordable and work using your existing Internet connectivity. And if you are ever in the position to have to get your files back from them, they will be worth every penny and more.

Speaking of locks, another kind of service provides you with a vault for secure, permanent storage of digital files but with a twist. **SwissDNABank.com** operates like a digital estate planning service, but also allows you to store a sample of your DNA. It's a way to actually store a piece of who you are. And for a one-time charge, they agree to store your DNA and data *forever*. It's an interesting proposition that you can promise data storage forever, much less store a DNA sample as well.

The Swiss DNA Bank promises perpetual storage of your data and a DNA sample.

What's Next?

These new and interesting services bring up another question: What's next? We're fairly certain that we'll see electronic death records in the future that will allow businesses to know when you've passed away. That might challenge your heirs' ability to access your accounts. Or perhaps it will motivate companies to ask what you want to happen to your accounts and automatically take those actions for you.

We're also wondering if we'll see digital cleaners in the future who will tidy up after you're gone to make sure your public image remains untarnished. Maybe they'll delete the online accounts you didn't want anyone to know about or make sure your online memorial is seeded with a few positive memories.

We also expect to see some of the technology's biggest players weigh in. Google, Yahoo, Apple, and Microsoft have all been relatively quiet about digital legacy. Once one of them takes a strong position, the others may follow.

What You Can Do

There are all sorts of opportunities coming from the industry to help you deal with digital death, but there's something you can do today. At this moment you hold all the access information for your digital assets, whether they're stored on your computer or on the Internet. You can leave it to your family and friends to pick up the pieces later, or you can invest in some planning now.

In the second section of this book we'll explain step by step what you can do today. By following our process, you'll complete an inventory of your digital assets, decide how you'd like them handled in the event of your death, and create a plan to pass them along to the next generation. We're not going to strong-arm you here, but think of the time, frustration, and cost you can save your heirs. And by helping them out, you might actually increase the chances that your wishes will be carried out and you'll achieve a meaningful digital afterlife.

*What you leave behind is not
what is engraved in stone monuments,
but what is woven into the lives of others.*
—PERICLES

SECURING YOUR
DIGITAL LEGACY

Quotation on page 96 is a concise translation of a passage in The Peloponnesian War *by Thucydides, Book II, Chapter 43, Section 3, from a speech by the Greek leader Pericles (ca. 495 BC–429 BC).*

CHAPTER 10

BEFORE YOU BEGIN

We understand that you've got lots of digital content and that it forms a rich digital identity that describes who you are. This content is probably important to you and to the people you know and will represent a legacy that can help future generations understand who you were.

If you've made it this far into the book you're probably more than convinced that you should take steps to secure this digital legacy. It's not too difficult, but it does take some organization and understanding.

Once you're done, you'll also have better control over your digital files and online accounts. You'll know where your content is and what your passwords are. You'll be better prepared for a catastrophic data loss (or the careless person at the coffeehouse who spills a latte on your laptop).

Your Digital Executor and Heirs

Throughout this section we will refer to your digital executor and heirs. It's important for you to understand how they are involved in your digital estate plan.

The digital executor will be a single person or a Web service of your choosing that will act objectively on your behalf after you are gone. Your digital executor will distribute or delete your digital assets according to your wishes. This role is central to the process since you won't be around to throw the switches yourself.

It's important to note that the executor defined in your legal will is the only person with true legal authority to settle your physical estate. Digital executors are not presently recognized by law. If your legal executor is capable, consider making your legal executor your digital executor also. Or consider adding your digital executor as a co-executor of your estate (just realize that co-executors have full legal authority over the whole estate). Both are good ways to empower your digital executor by law.

You may have one or more heirs for your assets. Heirs are the people who will be given your content and access to your accounts. The digital executor will be responsible for making heirs aware of accounts and content and will make sure that they have access to them. Your heirs will also carry out more specific instructions on your behalf, like posting a final tweet or maintaining your website.

Those of you with the simplest estates may appoint only one person (a spouse, for example) to be the legal executor, digital executor, and the sole heir. Good for you. That'll make things easier for everyone. But some of you may need finer control over your digital estate. In either case, the next few chapters can help.

Your Digital Assets

As we have talked about, there are many different types of digital assets. One of the most common types is digital files on your computer. Many are unimportant to future generations or to your digital legacy, but you'll need to make sure that your important assets are identified and preserved.

Next is your email, which represents not only your thoughts but entire conversations you have with others. You'll need to decide what email (if any) you want to preserve.

You also have online accounts. These accounts can contain digital files, conversations, and vital financial information. We'll help you identify your most important ones and help you preserve the most important aspects of each.

In the coming chapters we'll talk about these different kinds of digital assets and about providing your digital executor and heirs with the access they need to preserve them.

Access Equals Control

For the time being, access to an online account means you have control of the account. Online service providers do not (yet) have the ability to automatically find out when you pass away. That gives your digital executor an opportunity to carry out your wishes—but only if he or she has access. Over the next few chapters we'll help you provide that very control to your digital executor.

But we cannot expect this current state of affairs to last. It's only a matter of time before death records become digital. Once they do the Web will become "aware" of your death. That means companies will then know when you die and be able to automatically trigger processes outlined in their terms of service.

We'll talk more specifically about terms of service for email, online accounts, and financial accounts in the coming chapters.

Lack of Permanent Solutions

The idea of permanently storing all your data through time is intriguing (even if it sounds like something out of Star Trek). Unfortunately, as we mentioned in the previous chapter, there are issues concerning awareness, access, ownership, and preservation that must be addressed first. This section offers guidance to solve these problems.

At least for now, no matter how much you do, there are still systemic legal and preservation problems to be solved before you can say that anything you put in place is "permanent."

This leaves you to decide the fate of your assets in a situation in which things will change in the near future. So it's perfectly logical to ask yourself, "Why should I even bother?"

The good news is that we can expect progress in the next few years that will address the remaining problems. We can also expect greater awareness of the issues and hopefully some legal and technical standards. Technologists, archivists, and entrepreneurs are hard at work.

But without any plan, your digital content has very little chance of surviving. Even though that plan might only pass your digital content to your heirs, they may have the opportunity to make it permanent.

The Process

You should know that good organization and detailed planning are the secret sauce to securing your digital legacy. You need to inventory your assets, create your plan, and then set it into motion. We're going to help you through this—step by step.

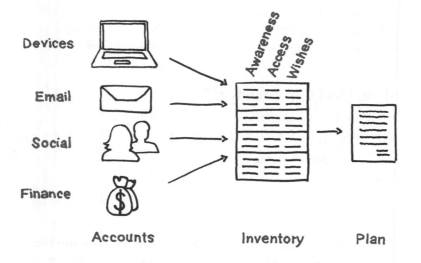

Your inventory worksheet will contain information about your digital assets and inform your digital estate plan.

What? More Work?

It's true that this can feel like work. But, **if you do nothing else, inventory your devices, your email, and your most important online accounts.** With that, your heirs will be able to capture, or at least piece together, the most important assets. To be sure that your digital content is taken care of, however, we recommend a more comprehensive list.

The first step to securing your digital legacy is to take an inventory of your digital assets. Provide the name, access, and wishes for each asset. Sounds easy, right? It may seem simple, but you probably have more digital files and online accounts than you think. By knowing and understanding the digital assets you have, you can make informed decisions about your wishes.

The second step is to make your plan. Once you have your inventory we'll talk about how to store and how to maintain it, and the trigger that releases it to your executor.

We'll talk about the common approaches that people take, including digital estate services, posthumous email services, and homegrown methods. We'll discuss the strengths and weaknesses of each and help you decide which to use. For people who need extra legal controls, we'll talk about ways to integrate with your legal will.

How Do I Get Started?

It's time to make your inventory. We'll create it by discussing the places where your digital content and online accounts are stored:

- Computers and other devices
- Email
- Social websites
- Financial and commerce accounts

For each type of asset we'll explain how to overcome the specific challenges of awareness and access and tell you about different wishes that are reasonable for each.

We recommend using a simple spreadsheet for your list. It should look something like this:

DIGITAL ASSET INVENTORY						
Asset		**Access**			**Wishes**	
Name	Contents	Location	User Name	Password	Instructions	Recipient

Go ahead and open Microsoft Excel, Google Docs, Apple Numbers, or whatever spreadsheet you like and get started. Don't have a spreadsheet program? There are free solutions that you can use like Google Docs (an online document management solution) or OpenOffice (a free suite of productivity tools).

We're all about making this process easier for you. That's why we developed a template for your inventory. To get started, visit **www .yourdigitalafterlife.com/resources** and download the blank tempate.

Quickstart Guide

Do you think instructions are for wimps? If you're the kind of person who assembles furniture without the manual, you may feel a need to jump right in. Download our inventory template and start filling it in. Make sure to list devices, email addresses, social website accounts, financial accounts, and anything else you think is important. When you're done, head over to Chapter 15, Create Your Plan.

Now that your spreadsheet is ready, let's make sure that your treasured assets can survive into the future. Ready. Go.

CHAPTER 11

COMPUTERS AND DEVICES

Desktops, laptops, mobile devices, tablets, music players—we access our digital assets using a variety of devices. As you plan for the digital afterlife, consider the contents of your devices first.

You use your devices to access two types of content—information that's stored locally on your computer and information that's stored elsewhere on the Internet. Five years ago most (if not all) of your content was stored on your devices, but today more and more of it is stored on the Internet. This might make you think that access to your computers and devices is less important now, but that's not the case. Access to them is essential for several reasons.

Access to computers, mobile devices, and tablets is essential in your planning.

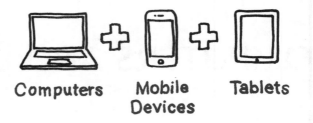

Computers   Mobile Devices   Tablets

Files on Devices

Computers and devices may contain important digital files that may not be on the Web or anywhere else. This makes your devices extremely important to the preservation of your digital assets.

But we need to think of devices and the digital files on them as two separate things. **A device is a single object that has to be given to one person. The files on it are part of your digital legacy and can be shared with many people. This means that you can consider the fate of the device and the files separately.**

In your inventory, you will need to record to whom the computer will physically be given. The digital executor will make sure that the heir has access to the machine. Once the heir has the machine and access to it, they will deal with the contents. In the simplest situation, you only have one heir and he or she is also your digital executor.

Master Keys on Devices

But your devices are more than a place for storing files. They can serve as a master key to your digital assets. As you create and interact with content stored in the cloud (somewhere on the Internet) you leave breadcrumbs on your device. This includes data like saved passwords, browsing history, and installed applications. If you didn't leave behind any other information for your heirs, it's from these breadcrumbs that they might start to piece things together. Of course, this book is about preventing them from having to do that.

So, when you think of the content on your devices, also think of its ability to provide access to other online content.

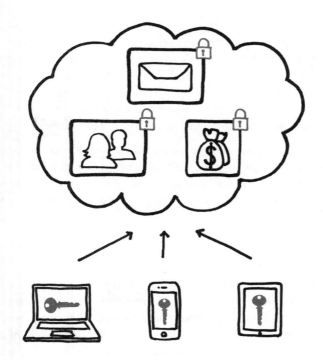

Your computers and devices serve as master keys to your email, social website accounts, and financial accounts.

The Law

An important distinction to be made here is that, unlike individual files and online accounts, computers and devices are considered tangible personal property by law and will be transferred along with your physical assets. This means you will need to specify who gets the hardware in your legal will. Don't have a will? Then your stuff will be distributed according to the laws of the state where it is located.

Also, some content on your device may not be transferable to your heirs. Digital rights managed (DRM) music is a good example. You didn't buy the music, you only bought the rights to listen.

Business Is Business

Many people wonder if they need to include their work computers in their inventory. You will if you have personal content on them. But be warned: Even though your employer may not take issue with you having personal files on your work computer, they may still deny your digital executor access to the machine or simply erase the files to prepare the device for someone else.

For this reason, it is recommended that you keep your personal assets on your personal devices. Now might be a good time to clear off your work computer and store your personal files, or at least those important to your legacy, somewhere else.

Backup

If no one has mentioned it lately, backing up your computer is incredibly important. All hard drives have a lifespan and will fail eventually. When they fail, it is difficult, expensive, and sometimes impossible to recover your data if you haven't backed it up. There are several ways to back up a hard drive. Choose a method and stick with it if you care about your data.

One way to back up your digital files is to burn them onto storage media like CDs and DVDs. This can be monumentally time consuming if you have a lot of content. A better way is to get a second hard drive and use software to synchronize the two drives with each other. This is much easier for large collections of digital files and has prevented thousands of people from losing all their data. You can automate the process so it happens regularly and automatically.

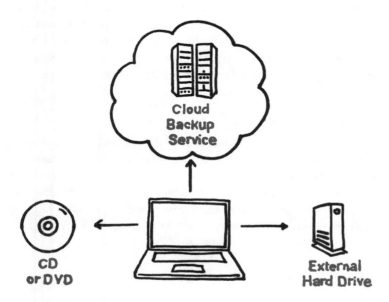

You can back up files to online services, external drives, optical media, or a combination thereof.

Many people have begun to back up their computers to online backup services. These services are fantastic protection against the inevitable hard drive failure and even a house fire since your data isn't only in your own home. These services are also excellent ways to protect all your data for your loved ones. Just remember to add these accounts to your list. Here are a few common ones:

- www.mozy.com
- www.idrive.com
- www.sosonlinebackup.com
- www.carbonite.com
- www.sugarsync.com

Awareness

The first step in passing on any device is to make sure that your digital executor is aware that it exists. Start by recording each device on your inventory sheet.

But each of your computers and devices is also a container for many types of digital content. If you want the files to also go to the heir of the device, you may be done. Then again, you may not have the same wishes for the entire contents of a device. In this case, you'll need to decide whether to subdivide your wishes for a particular device.

Adult Content?

Some people have content that is, shall we say, "private." It's quite possible that you don't want your spouse, children, or your parents to find this content. If so, specifying an digital executor or heir who can delete your "adult content" collection from your machine will be important to you. We know it may be taboo to talk about, but this content will most certainly be found if you don't do anything.

Take Action   *Awareness*

Go ahead and record the name of your computers and devices now. Also list any backup hard drives or services that you are using.

Below each device, list groups or types of files (or even super important individual files) that you want treated differently on separate lines. Your inventory will look something like this:

ASSET		ACCESS			WISHES		
Name	**Contents**	**Location**	**User Name**	**Password**	**Instructions**	**Heir**	**Notes**
Home laptop							
	Home movies, photos						
	Adult content						
Phone							
	Photos						

Remember, we have an inventory template available at **www.yourdigitalafterlife.com/resources**.

Access

For your devices, access has two components: their physical location and the credentials (usually a user name and password, but sometimes just a password) needed to log into them. As your estate is settled, your digital executor will provide your heirs with the credentials that they will need to access your devices. Once the heir has the physical device and access to it, he or she will be able to carry out your wishes.

Physical Location

Your computers might be at your home or office and your mobile devices will probably be in your pocket or a bag. You'll want to make sure that your executor can find them. If they are under lock and key, be sure to make a note of how to gain physical access to them.

Passwords

Devices without a password are simply a power switch away, but many of your devices will be protected by a password. You have a few options for helping your heirs gain access. Each of these options has inherent advantages and disadvantages.

With all of this planning for death, you should remember the reason you have a password in the first place. It's to keep your information private and secure. Depending on the option you choose, you may undermine the security of your devices during your life, so be careful. You've been warned.

Leave Your Password

The simplest option is to leave your password for your heir. This option is probably easiest for them, but has a few disadvantages. For those of you who change your passwords often, you'll need to get into the habit of updating your documents for your digital executor.

Depending on how you choose to leave this information for them, doing this may require vigilance (we'll talk about the choices in Chapter 15, Create Your Plan). With this option you also won't know if someone else has accessed your device, which is good information to have.

For better or worse, this is the only option for some devices. For example, the screen lock on iOS devices (iPhone, iPad, and iPod) cannot be reset without deleting all information on the device if you don't have the existing password. For these devices you might want to leave your password in a secure place.

Reset Your Password

For some devices, leaving a way to reset your password is a viable option. This is possible with nearly every type of personal computer. Remember, however, that this process is about making things easier for your heirs and there are a few options to reset a password easily. You may want to leave instructions for how to use the DVD.

The Windows operating system allows you to create a password reset disk on on external storage like a USB drive. Creating and providing a password reset disk to an heir will allow them to login and create a new password, without knowing your old password. This is a good solution if you like to change your password often.

For Mac OS X you don't even need a special disk. You can use the Mac OS X DVD to reset the password on any Mac running that operating system. You may want to leave instructions for how to do this.

Realize that with the right tools and technical understanding, it is even possible to reset a password without your prior planning or authorization. We won't go into the details of doing that reset here, but a quick Web search will point you in the right direction.

Make an Additional Account

Another tactic is to create an additional user account with administrative access. You can then leave the password to that account in your records and continue to change your everyday account password as needed. This is another good option if you like to change your password often, but could compromise your present-day security if someone gains access to this new account.

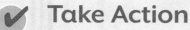 **Take Action**

Make note of how your digital executor will access your device. Record any relevant locations, user names, and passwords.

ASSET		ACCESS			WISHES		
Name	**Contents**	**Location**	**User Name**	**Password**	**Instructions**	**Heir**	**Notes**
Home laptop		At home	joesmith	myC0mpuTer!			
	Home movies, photos						
	Adult content						
Phone		Usually in pocket	None	5514			
	Photos						

Remember, we have an inventory template available at **www.yourdigitalafterlife.com/resources**.

Wishes

Your next step is to determine what instructions you want your heirs to follow for each of your computers and devices. It's important to understand the options you have here so you can set realistic wishes.

The heir will be the person who has physical ownership of the device. This is why we say that the heir will be the person to carry out your wishes. But your digital executor may be the person who has the technical ability to carry out your wishes. In this case you may consider leaving your devices to your digital executor or working out a plan where the heir and digital executor will work together to carry out your wishes.

Your Heirs

Consider to whom you want to leave your content. Once you know that, you'll be able to provide the appropriate instructions for your digital executor.

Typical choices might be

- One person: your spouse, your child
- Group: parents, close family, friends

- Everyone: Maybe you want to put it out there for the world.
- No one: Some things are best not shared. 'Nuff said.

Your Instructions

Now let's talk about what you want to happen to your content. You will see that there's a relationship between the heir you choose and the instructions you leave.

Archive the Content

To archive your data, your heir will need to create a copy of the content and place it on some sort of media (like a CD, DVD, USB drive, or external hard drive). This process can be a lot of work, but it might be appropriate for some types of content. Keep in mind that having multiple copies of your archive keeps it better protected from loss and sharing it among several people may increase the likelihood of it being preserved.

Share the Content

You may want the contents of your device to go to more than one individual, which leads us to sharing the contents with a larger group, or even the world. It probably doesn't make sense to share the entire contents of your device, but chances are good that many people in your life might want a copy of things like photos and movies. There are several ways to accomplish this.

One way is to have the heir take the digital content from your device and place it on the Internet. Depending on the exact content we're talking about, a bit of formatting and organization might be required.

Another way would be to put them on multiple CDs, DVDs, or USB drives and send them to all the people you want to share them with.

Delete the Content

Deletion is a good way to deal with content that's personal and not really for anyone else to see. This is a fairly straightforward process on a device in contrast to what you might have to do on the Internet (as we will see in later chapters). No doubt you've experienced accidental deletion and understand this very well. If deletion is on your mind, you'll want to specify exactly what to delete, whether it is the entire computer or just specific content.

For example, a relative of mine who has specified me as her digital executor has asked me to delete the contents of her computer following her death. I even have a key to her residence to ensure that this happens. But I'm supposed to save all of her photos first, because those are of great value to the family. It's plans like these that allow you to protect your privacy while still sharing valuable content. It simply takes organization, planning, and leaving specific instructions for your digital executors.

Do Nothing

Strange as it may sound, you may decide to do nothing at all. Realize that if you do nothing you are letting whatever happens happen. But this is an option for people who share a computer with another person and don't need to tell them what to do.

Now all of your devices are recorded in your digital asset inventory, and you're one step closer to securing your digital legacy. Next we'll talk about the other master key to your digital content, your email.

 ## Take Action   *Wishes*

Decide what you would like to happen to your devices and their contents. Add additional lines to your document to account for dividing up content from a specific device.

ASSET		ACCESS			WISHES		
Name	**Contents**	**Location**	**User Name**	**Password**	**Instructions**	**Heir**	**Notes**
Home laptop		At home	joesmith	myC0mpuTer!			
	Home movies, photos				Share	Family	
	Adult content				Delete	No one	
Phone		Usually in pocket	None	5514			
	Photos				Share	Family, friends	

Remember, we have an inventory template available at **www.yourdigitalafterlife.com/resources**.

CHAPTER 12

EMAIL

Email is as important, if not more important, than your computers and devices. Even with the advent of Facebook, Twitter, and SMS messaging, email continues to retain a prominent role. In fact, four of the top fifteen most popular sites on the Internet are Web-based email sites.

As the most ubiquitous form of electronic communication, your email address serves as your unique identifier on the Internet. From a planning standpoint, it serves as another master key to your digital content. For most online accounts you receive an email message when you sign up. If you save these messages, you have a record of the account's existence and perhaps the user name or password. But since email is a unique identifier, your heirs could probably use your email account to recover your user name or reset your password.

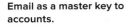

Email as a master key to accounts.

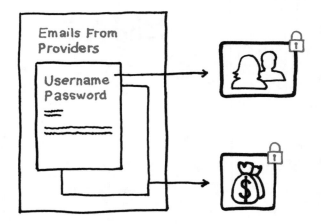

But email is much more than a way to reset and retrieve passwords. If you put aside all the spam and notifications, you'll find a few gems. Documented conversations between you and the people you care about: Your writings, and how your friends and family respond, create a rich picture of you, your thoughts, and your life. And that's way more important than a unique identifier.

It might be safe to say that *you* are what's in your email. And to your grieving family, that may be just what they need. In Chapter 2, The Shift to Digital, we talked about Justin Ellsworth, who was killed by a roadside bomb in Fallujah, Iraq, and how his father, John, worked to get access to his son's email.

John Ellsworth is not the only person with this story. We've read countless others like his, except that he had the resolve to take the issue to the courts and win. Your survivors may not have the means to do the same. So let's keep that from happening.

Terms of Service

Before we go any further, let's pause to discuss the legal issues at hand. If you host your own email server, you probably don't have terms of service and won't have legal issues to deal with. But a vast majority of people use services provided by an Internet Service Provider (ISP), like AT&T, Comcast, Road Runner, or Verizon, or a Web-based email provider, like Yahoo Mail, Microsoft Live, or Gmail. All of these are governed by a terms of service agreement.

When you signed up for your email account, you agreed to the terms of service. It's usually a check box near the end of the form. And when you checked it, you probably did not read through the legalese. Chances are high that the agreement said something about "transferability" and "termination," but probably nothing about death or survivorship. And that's a problem.

With no mention of death in these agreements, and no standards for dealing with the issue, you can't be sure what will happen when you pass away. To add to the confusion, there are no state or federal laws that have definitively answered the question of the rights of heirs to email. In fact, the law isn't even sure that email can be considered property.

We often don't consider what happens to these accounts until it's too late. Consider John Ellsworth, mentioned above. He got a court to order Yahoo to give him copies of the emails in his son's account, but Yahoo hasn't changed its terms. The terms still state that accounts are nontransferable (to an heir) and that Yahoo has the right to delete everything in an account upon the user's death. That sounds a bit harsh, but you may have agreed to just that unknowingly.

But there's good news. By recording your email accounts in your inventory, you can work around this limitation.

Awareness

As before, the first step to securing your email accounts is to make sure that your digital executor knows about them. Your email address itself actually provides a lot of information about the account, but there are all sorts of complexities with email accounts. The more information you can provide about your email account, the less guesswork you'll leave for your digital executor.

Simply put, an email account is like a post office box. It's a place where messages are sent and stored until you access them. Email addresses direct messages to a specific server on the Internet that's indicated by the part of your email address following the @ symbol. It's useful to understand and record who owns the server that hosts your email. You may have email accounts hosted by your Internet provider or a Web-based email service. Or you may use a privately hosted email server from your company, school, or other organization.

Don't Mix Business with Pleasure

Do you have personal messages in your work email? This is a monumentally bad idea unless you happen to own your own company. Most companies have their own policies concerning termination, and many delete or cut access to accounts the moment you no longer work there. It's not meant to be mean, but they need to ensure that important emails aren't missed. So do yourself a favor: Keep important personal content out of work email. It's as simple as hitting the forward button and continuing the conversation from your personal account.

Now that you understand a few things about email accounts, you'll want to provide the appropriate information about them for your heirs. The more information you provide the better, but at the very least you should record your address, who owns the email server, and the types of messages stored there.

Be sure to remember accounts you just use for junk mail or accounts that you no longer use. Sometimes online accounts are linked to these email addresses.

Record each email account on your inventory list. Use the Name column for your address and to describe who hosts the email account. Use the Contents column to describe of what kind of messages are stored there.

| ASSET | | ACCESS | | | WISHES | | |
Name	Contents	Location	User Name	Password	Instructions	Heir	Notes
joe.smith@gmail.com Gmail	Emails about hobbies, interests						
joe.smith@att.com AT&T	Junk email						
joesmith@me.com MobileMe/Apple	Personal email						

Remember, we have an inventory template available at **www.yourdigitalafterlife.com/resources**.

Access

Before we go any further, you should know that there are different types of email. How you access and store your email will determine the information you need to leave your heirs. It could be as simple as leaving access to your computer. But it could also involve lots of technical details about your email servers, user names, and passwords.

As we said earlier, incoming messages arrive at an email server and are kept there for you. The differences have to do with how you access these messages and what happens to them after you do so. Just to make things more complicated, you may access your email in multiple ways. You could, for instance, access your email on both your mobile phone and your computer. Let's look at the ways you may access your email.

Desktop Software
Many people use desktop applications like Windows Mail, Mail (for Mac), or Mozilla Thunderbird to send, read, and store email. This method downloads or synchronizes messages to your computer from

the email server. There is a possibility that your desktop software erases the messages off the server once it downloads them. In this case, your device has the sole copy of the email. Many of these applications have built-in ways to archive your mail to disk so you can copy it to a backup location.

Mobile Devices

If you check email on your mobile device you may be using the built-in email application for iOS, Android, or BlackBerry. Typically these devices store email on your device, but leave a copy on the server so you can download the message to your computer as well. Make sure that you have a backup elsewhere, because mobile devices generally do not have a way to archive messages.

Webmail

Webmail allows you to manage email using your Internet browser. When mail is accessed this way, the mail is never downloaded or synced to your computer. Instead, the messages are stored on the email server. Once you close your browser, no email remains on your machine. You'll likely be checking your email in a Web browser like Firefox, Safari, Google Chrome, or Internet Explorer.

Types of email accounts.

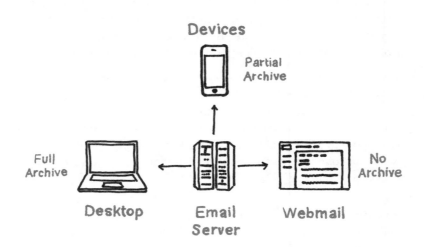

Regardless of how you access your email, record the server location, user name, and password for the account. If you use email software, your digital executor will already have access, if you listed your computers and devices in the previous chapter. But even if you did, it will be beneficial to document all the necessary locations, user names, and passwords. After all, your devices could become damaged before or after your death.

A "Permanent" Email?

People change their ISPs often. What many forget is that email accounts at ISPs are routinely deleted when accounts are closed.

If you care about archiving your email this may present a challenge, especially if you use webmail, since you won't have any of your email stored on your device. In this case you would have to archive your mail using desktop software before closing your account.

If you use your ISP's email, consider transferring to a more portable email provider like Gmail or Yahoo. Using an email service that is independent of your hosting service will allow you to change ISPs without having to deal with loss of email.

Regardless of whom you use to host your email, you will need to consider how your email is accessed and stored if you want to archive it.

Location

Write down where your email server is located. For desktop software and mobile devices, record the incoming mail server. If you're not sure of it, you can find that in the account settings in your email software. If you use webmail all you'll need is the URL where you check your mail. For example if you use Gmail, you'll record https://mail.google.com.

User Name

Next, list your user name. This will likely be your entire email address or just the first part. It is possible to have a different user name as well. If your email provider uses an additional user name (other than email address), record that here.

Password

Passwords are fairly straightforward and all email accounts have them. If you use webmail, record the password that you enter each time you open your email account.

If you use email software, you probably don't enter your password regularly. If you're unsure of your password, you may be able to view it in your account settings. If not, you'll need to contact your email provider and reset it. Once you know your password, record it in your inventory.

Optional Notes

It will be helpful for your digital executor to know how you access your email, whether it's via software, a mobile device, webmail, or a combination thereof. Use the Notes column to record that information.

If your desktop software contains the only copy of your email, make a note so that your digital executor knows that he or she needs the physical device to access your email. Look in your account settings. If you are using a "POP3" protocol, check to see if your software is set to remove copies from the server after retrieving messages. If that's the case, your desktop software contains the only copy of your email.

✔ Take Action   *Access*

Record the location, user name, password, and access note in your inventory.

ASSET		ACCESS			WISHES		
Name	**Contents**	**Location**	**User Name**	**Password**	**Instructions**	**Heir**	**Notes**
joe.smith@ gmail.com Gmail	Emails about hobbies, interests	mail.google.com	joe-smith@ gmail.com	G0J0e!0415			Webmail
joe.smith@att.com AT&T	Junk email	mail.att.com	joe-smith1201@ att.com	cupAj03			Software: Apple Mail
joesmith@me.com MobileMe/Apple	Personal email	me.com	jsmith@me.com	GljOe!sThere			Mobile, Webmail

Remember, we have an inventory template available at **www.yourdigitalafterlife.com/resources**.

Wishes

The final step is to record your wishes for your email accounts. As with your computers and devices, your wishes include both your instructions and the heir of the account.

Instructions

Consider what you want to happen to each item on your list. Here you have several options and can even combine options should you desire.

Archive It

Like your hard drive, you may want to archive your email. Again, this will mean that the data is copied onto a hard drive or storage media (like a CD or DVD).

Some desktop programs like Mac Mail or Microsoft Outlook have built-in archive utilities that allow you to archive and back up your mail. Just place the exported archive files on a CD, DVD, hard drive, or other media. Other programs require you to find where the mail is stored on the machine and back it up manually.

Not sure how to archive the email in your software? We can't cover all the possibilities here, but a quick Web or help menu search should help you find the answer.

Webmail and mobile devices are a bit harder. To archive them you'll need to set up an email client on your computer and download or sync the mail to that machine (using POP or IMAP). Then archive the mail using the desktop software.

Share It

Sharing your email sounds nice, but it's tricky business because half of "your" email is really other people's email. Remember, they are still alive, so be considerate. You could hurt people's feelings by sharing too much.

You could ask your digital executor or heir to save out copies of email from or to specific people. This is a nice way to share your thoughts with special people but it can take a lot of time, so be realistic with his or her time.

Giving wide access to your webmail account is a bad idea because of all the personal, financial, and account information that may be stored there. You could inadvertently give everyone access to reset your bank account password.

Delete It

Deletion of accounts it often easy, just make sure that you don't need the account anymore. Often an online account can only be accessed using a specific (valid) email address.

You may want to have your digital executor delete emails to or from certain people or from certain services or websites. Now we're not trying to help you lie or deceive, but there are documented accounts of marital affairs being discovered by the email trails left behind. We could talk more about the accuracy of your legacy, but we'll put that aside for now. Consider this fair warning to tie up your loose ends.

Leave It Alone

If you have a family account that many people share, there may not be much to do. Just make sure that your digital executor knows not to close down the email.

Auto Responses

Most email services and many email programs allow you to set up auto responses. These are most often used when business people are out of the office for some time. You may ask your digital executor to set up an auto responder to inform people of your passing. After all you'll be, well, out of the office. It's also helpful for your heir as he or she might not have to check the box as often.

You could leave a message such as:

> **This email address is longer being checked regularly because Joe Smith is no longer alive. Please send any condolences to his family at thesmiths@att.com.**

Or, you could leave a less formal email like:

> **This is embarrassing, but I'm not alive anymore. It's been a great ride. Peace out —Joe**

Forward New Messages

Sometimes an email is connected to an organization or another person who needs access to the email account. Maybe you want your spouse to answer your email for a while so that he or she can respond to friends and family. Maybe work emails should be forwarded to a business partner to deal with.

Posthumous Email

There are services that will host emails that you want sent out after you die. We'll talk more about that in Chapter 15, Create Your Plan. Stay tuned.

Send Your Drafts

You may decide to write some emails to your loved ones and put them in your draft folder. This allows you to say things you wish you would have said, remind people that you love them, or get in the last word. If you create emails like this, leave your digital executor a note to send these drafts to the proper recipients.

Email from the Dead

When it comes to posthumous email, be aware that email penned by the author before he or she dies is fine. But penning email in a deceased person's name is weird and potentially hurtful. Don't do it, please.

Hybrids

Some of these options deal with existing emails and others with new ones you'll send or receive. You can actually combine several of these options, as long as you write specific instructions and are careful not to specify opposing wishes. For example, you may instruct your heir to archive your messages and then forward new ones. Or you might ask that they delete old messages and set up an auto responder to future messages.

Define a Heir

As you consider this, also think about who the heir is. It may simply be your digital executor or your spouse, or it could be a group or everyone. Different wishes have different possible heirs. This list shows the different heirs for each instruction:

INSTRUCTIONS	HEIRS
Archive	One or more people who should receive the entire archive.
Share	One or more people to receive copies of all or part of your emails.
Delete	No heir
Leave it alone	No heir
Auto response	One person to set up the auto responder and the message you'd like for them to send.
Forward	The person who should receive new messages and their email address.
Send drafts	Each person for whom you've prepared a message.

Now you have a handle on your email accounts. If you stop here, it's likely that your heirs will have access to most, if not all, of your digital assets. That said, you probably want to have a say in what happens to these assets, so you'll want to think about the accounts you have at various social websites next.

Take Action

Write your wishes for each email account.

ASSET		ACCESS			WISHES		
Name	**Contents**	**Location**	**User Name**	**Password**	**Instructions**	**Heir**	**Notes**
joe.smith@ gmail.com Gmail	Emails about hobbies, interests	mail.google.com	joe-smith@ gmail.com	G0J0e!0415	Forward to Jane Smith; delete old messages	Jane Smith	Webmail
joe.smith@ att.com AT&T	Junk email	mail.att.com	joe-smith1201@ att.com	cupAj03	Delete	No one	Software: Apple Mail
joesmith@ me.com MobileMe/ Apple	Personal email	me.com	jsmith@me.com	GljOe!sThere	Archive messages	Jane, Paul, and Tasha	Mobile, Webmail

Remember, we have an inventory template available at **www.yourdigitalafterlife.com/resources**.

CHAPTER 13

SOCIAL WEBSITES

It would be an understatement to say that social, or "Web 2.0," web-sites are an increasing part of our lives. We use sites like Facebook, Flickr, and Twitter everyday. These sites have changed so much about how we interact culturally that entire books are devoted to the topic. We can't cover the cultural issues here, but it's important to under-stand how much content we create on social websites and exactly how important they are in our lives.

As today's most popular social website, let's use Facebook as an example. With over 500 million users, Facebook has more users than the entire population of the United States. In fact, if Facebook were a country, it would be the third largest in the world. Some fancy math using age groups, death rates, and Facebook data tells us that over 285,000 U.S. Facebook users will pass away in 2010. Any other social website faces the same problems.

In terms of population, Facebook would be the third-largest country in the world.

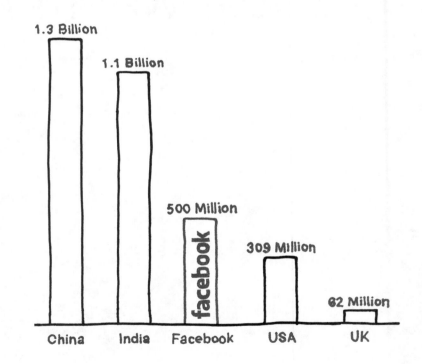

1.3 Billion — China
1.1 Billion — India
500 Million — Facebook
309 Million — USA
62 Million — UK

So what are these deceased users leaving behind? Depending on the social network, they could leave status updates, messages, photos, videos, and conversations. Even more importantly, they leave behind connections between individuals who might not be connected otherwise.

CONTENT	SITES
Connections, messages	Facebook, MySpace, Orkut, LinkedIn
Photos	Flickr, Facebook, Picasa, Snapfish, Photobucket
Videos	YouTube, Vimeo, Flickr, Facebook
Writings or blog articles	WordPress, Blogger, TypePad, LiveJournal
Short messages	Twitter, Tumblr
Check-ins, messages	Foursquare, Gowalla, Facebook, Brightkite

Chances are good you use many of these social sites on a regular basis. And you publish content there because you want to share it with a wider audience like your friends or even the entire world. Considering the care that you've taken to create and curate this content, you should plan for its legacy.

In this section we will add your social accounts to your inventory. This will enable your digital executor to make your recipients aware of your accounts and provide the recipients access to them.

Awareness

We've said a few times that you need to make your digital executor aware of your digital assets so he or she can carry out your wishes. The same is true of the content you store in social sites. The good news is that many of your friends and family members may already be aware of these accounts because you created them so you could connect with—you guessed it—family and friends.

Despite that fact, you should still include them in your inventory. Doing so will enable you to specify wishes other than what will naturally happen. Later in this chapter we'll talk about some sites that have a policy for deceased users and what you can expect if you don't take action.

You should also consider that you may interact with a different group of people online than you do in real life. Or your survivors may not have had contact with particular online accounts. In fact, you probably have online accounts that you've forgotten about. Three more reasons why you should inventory them. Ready yet?

But Wait, I Have a Lot of Accounts

Anyone who spends an appreciable amount of time on the Internet faces the same problem. But that's okay. We're going to help you organize them. The fact remains, however, that some accounts will be more valuable to you than others. As this point it makes sense to make note of them all and we'll address value as you determine your wishes.

 ## Take Action   *Awareness*

Record all your social website accounts in your inventory. Go ahead and complete the Name and Contents columns.

ASSET		ACCESS			WISHES	
Name	Contents	Location	User Name	Password	Instructions	Recipient
Facebook	Messages, Photos					
Twitter	Tweets					
Flickr	Photos					
MySpace	Some photos, old messages					

Remember, we have an inventory template available at **www.yourdigitalafterlife.com/resources**.

Access

Just as you can access most of your online accounts from anywhere, so can your survivors. To provide access, you just need to provide the URL of the account, user name, and password. When doing this, consider two things:

1. Many services place a nontransferability clause in the terms of service. These terms basically state that you cannot transfer your account to another person. We'll talk more about this later in the chapter.

2. Whoever has access to the email account you used to create this particular online account probably has the ability to reset the password. If you need to divide your assets between two people, and discretion is essential, you'll want to consider this fact.

If you're not comfortable with providing someone with direct access, you can consider ways to back up the content from one service to another. For example, you may not want to leave access to your Flickr account, but you could place all of the photo files on a backup service and provide your heirs with access to that service.

Facebook and Twitter as Master Keys

Increasingly websites are allowing you to authenticate using Facebook and Twitter. These sites may soon serve as master keys much like email.

Some services, especially content publishing services, are designed to let you share content publicly on the Web. In some cases you might want to allow your heirs to access your blog just like any other reader, but not give them the credentials to post. In this case, access can be achieved by simply leaving a URL.

A Word about Websites (Experts Only Please)

Maybe you're a little more savvy and you have a website with your own domain name. Consider for a moment how your heirs will deal with the complexities. You're probably aware of the interconnected nature of email, domain registration, DNS, and Web hosting. You also know that if any of these services gets disabled, everything may stop working. So leaving out any of these pieces from your inventory can cause mass mayhem.

For example, if you neglect to specify your registrar and your heirs let your domain registration lapse, your email and website will go down. Plus domain registration can't be changed unless you have access to the email address named on the registrar account.

Make sure you have a technically savvy person lined up to help with these types of accounts. Leave them all the necessary information. It's also a good idea to leave a few notes on how you have everything configured, so they won't have to spend too much time figuring it out.

✔ Take Action   *Access*

Record the user names and passwords along with URLs for each of your social websites.

ASSET		ACCESS			WISHES	
Name	Contents	Location	User Name	Password	Instructions	Recipient
Facebook	Messages, Photos	www.facebook.com	joe.smith@email.com	cobraB!tes!		
Twitter	Tweets	www.twitter.com/joe	Joe	J0ein140		
Flickr	Photos	www.flickr.com/photos/15140142@N03	Joe_Smith	Sh0tsOjoe		
MySpace	Some photos, old messages	www.myspace.com/joerocks	Joerocks	My5p@c3		

Remember, we have an inventory template available at **www.yourdigitalafterlife.com/resources**.

Wishes

With online accounts, you may have several different wishes, but you should first consider whom the recipient should be. This person (or people) will receive access to the account from the digital executor.

You may decide that there is *no* recipient for some accounts. You may choose to ask your digital executor to delete the account for you without handing it on to anyone. This is a great option for accounts that you never really used or don't want kicking around after you're gone.

While your digital executor may be a person, it can also be a Web service. One such service, Entrustet, has a feature called the Account Incinerator. It will delete unwanted accounts without anyone being the wiser.

But before you delete an account or change people's access to it, consider that your content or profile is often linked to other people's accounts. Consider how your friends may feel when your content suddenly disappears!

Leave It in Place

The simplest thing you can do is leave an online account in place without any changes. Your online friends might actually find it comforting to see something remain exactly as you've left it, especially for situations where it might be awkward for someone else to take over for you. Twitter is a good example of this. Brad Graham was well-known among Internet professionals when he passed away in 2009. His Twitter account has remained unchanged since that time (see illustration on next page), and many of his followers continued to mention him in their Tweets for some time after.

Provide Resolution

Although leaving something alone may seem like the right thing to do, you may want to let people know that you have passed away. This fact is especially relevant in an online community where there are no real-life interactions (i.e., where your physical death isn't obvious).

We've heard many stories about members of Second Life (a 3D virtual community) who have passed away and their online friends didn't know about it for several months. To them, their friend suddenly disappeared and they were left to ask if they had done something to drive them away.

Brad Graham's Twitter profile, unchanged since December 2009.

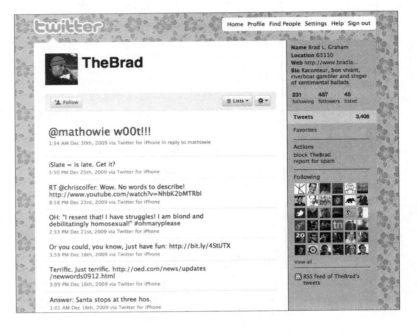

So in the Twitter example above, you could leave instructions for your digital executor to log in and leave your last tweet. This fits well within 140 characters:

> **It's been real, friends. See you on the other side. Cheers.**

Let It Grow

With some assets like websites and blogs it makes sense to allow someone else to continue writing and creating for you. This process is more involved than simply providing resolution; it requires a commitment from your "blog heir" to continue creating content and extending your legacy.

This is especially appropriate for blogs that have gained a following and serve as a community for others. For example, Lisa Kelly from Clusterfook.com died of ovarian cancer in February 2009. She gave her friend Karl administrative access to her blog so that he could notify readers of her death and publish her final post. He also posts periodic updates from her family. From the comments on her site you can tell that her readers deeply cared for her and her family. Karl's work to keep everyone connected is a wonderful tribute to her legacy. Unfortunately Clusterfook.com went offline as we were writing the book.

RIP Lisa Clusterfook

by SECONDHAND KARL *on* FEBRUARY 28, 2009
in CANCER SUCKS

Just got the call from Dude. Lisa died about 45 minutes ago, at around 11:30 PM Friday night. He's frazzled, but is thankful she's not in pain any more.

RIP, Lisa. You're missed already.

◀ ShareThis

Tagged as: cancer blows, Cancer Sucks, Clusterfook, Lisa, RIP

Lisa Kelly's death announcement from Clusterfook.com.

Memorialize It

When someone passes away, there's a need for their friends and family to grieve together. Social networking sites have become a location for that communal bereavement. It's actually quite fascinating to see a group of otherwise unconnected individuals come together to mourn their lost friend. It's even more special for those memories to be preserved long after the typical grieving period marked by a funeral or wake.

Facebook has recognized the need for friends to grieve together. Originally they left the profiles of the deceased unchanged. Eventually they launched new site features to help people connect with new friends and reconnect with friends that are inactive. This led to a lot of situations where survivors were being asked to reconnect with deceased friends and loved ones. These persistent reminders of loss were unwelcome by many and caused a good deal of hurt.

In response to this issue and in an attempt to foster communal grieving, Facebook decided to create a memorialized status for profiles. A memorialized profile is like any other Facebook profile, but the account can no longer be accessed with a user name and password. To protect the privacy of the deceased, contact information and status updates are also removed. The Wall remains open for preexisting Facebook friends to post memories.

Anyone who can prove you've passed away with a death certificate or obituary can request that your profile be memorialized. So, it would be difficult for your digital executor to prevent this from happening. You'll want to ensure that your wall posts are saved elsewhere should you want them to be preserved.

Archive It

As with computers, you can also download and archive the contents of your social websites. This would be appropriate if you wanted to share the content with your family or a few friends, but remove it from the eyes of the world.

Report a Deceased Person's Profile

IMPORTANT: This form is solely for the reporting of a deceased person to memorialize or remove the person's account. Memorializing the account removes certain sensitive information and sets privacy so that only confirmed friends can see the profile or locate it in search. The Wall remains so that friends and family can leave posts in remembrance. Please note that unrelated inquiries through this form may not receive a response.

Your email address:
The email address where you can be reached. If you are able to access your login email address, enter that here.

Full Name:
on the account

Date of birth: Month: ▼ Day: ▼ Year: ▼

Account email addresses:
which may have been used to create the account

Networks:
which the person may have been in (e.g., the Stanford University educational network)

Web address (URL) of the profile you would like to report:
Please copy and paste the web address (URL) of his/her profile.

Relationship to the person: Please select: ▼

Requested action: Please select: ▼

Proof of death:
an obituary or news article

Additional relevant information:

Submit   Cancel

The form anyone can complete to memorialize a Facebook profile.

Every social site is different and archiving your content from them ranges from easy to super difficult. There is also the ownership issue. Again, Facebook provides a good example. You may post content from the Web to your Wall, but that doesn't imply ownership over the content. Or maybe you have a conversation about someone else's photo that you are tagged in. Do you "own" that photo? Can you rightfully archive that content?

For the time being, access to content enables you to archive it (although it may be against the terms of service). There are several tools to help you or your digital executors make an archive. We've included an index of tools for archiving content from several popular social sites in Appendix B.

Delete It

It's always a good idea to carefully consider when you want to delete something, but sometimes it is the best option. With social websites, deletion is actually a complicated process. Many of these sites have business models that depend on having users. They'll do everything they can to keep their users around. Some sites will archive your content just in case you want to come back later.

Should you choose to delete an account you should look to the help section of that site or search the Internet for instructions on deleting it. These processes change all the time, but are well recorded by different people as they go through the process.

Alignment with Terms of Service

We mentioned above that in some cases the terms of service dictate what should happen upon your death, regardless of your wishes. Before we ask you to record those, you should review these terms to make sure that your wishes align.

When you create or upload content to these sites, you are placing it on servers that you do not own. For example, if you upload photos to Flickr you're physically placing them on servers owned by Yahoo (which owns Flickr) in one of their data centers.*

Isn't that nice of Yahoo? Well, yes and no. They provide you with a great service for sharing your photos and even allow you do to so at little to no cost. But when you first create your account you agree to Yahoo's terms of service. This legal document will vary from site to site, but generally states what you give the site and what they will give you in return.

This document is a legally binding agreement that governs your relationship with them. Many social websites do not include provisions for your death in the terms of service, but some, like Yahoo, do. As you consider what you wish to happen to your social web content, you have to take this into consideration. The terms of service at each site will determine how you can provide access to your digital executor and what wishes are reasonable for you to expect.

---

*The example terms of service quoted here were current at the time of writing, but are primarily for the purposes of discussion. Companies may change their terms of service at any time.

The Fine Print

One thing to consider is that giving another individual access to your account may in itself be a breach of the terms of service. There are no legal precedents to say whether a legal executor should have the right to access an account, but doing so could technically serve as the grounds for termination of the right to use the service.

This is a catch-22. If you don't provide access, your heirs would lose the content; if you do, the account could be terminated. But it's not likely that a service will find out, and by providing access the content becomes accessible.

We believe that your heirs should have the rights to your content, but unfortunately we don't make the rules.

Here's a quick glance at what some popular social sites have in their terms of service regarding death.

Facebook covers the rights of deceased users in their privacy policy:

> Memorializing Accounts. If we are notified that a user is deceased, we may memorialize the user's account. In such cases we restrict profile access to confirmed friends, and allow friends and family to write on the user's Wall in remembrance. We may close an account if we receive a formal request from the user's next of kin or other proper legal request to do so.

So for Facebook, it's reasonable for you to request that your account be deleted or that it be left in a memorial state. It's not possible for it to stay active, as anyone can request that it be memorialized by simply notifying Facebook and showing a death certificate or news article that indicates your death.

Gmail provides instructions for gaining access to deceased user's account in their help documents. They outline the steps to gaining access, which include a death certificate, and email you have received from the account in question and proof that you have legal authority over the estate.

Twitter also addresses this issue in their help documents:

> If we are notified that a Twitter user has passed away, we can remove their account or assist family members in saving a backup of their public Tweets.

> Please contact us with the following information:

> 1. Your full name, contact information (including email address), and your relationship to the deceased user.
> 2. The username of the Twitter account, or a link to the profile page of the Twitter account.
> 3. A link to a public obituary or news article.

Twitter is unique in that they offer survivors an archive of the user's public Tweets. That's very helpful as it's often difficult to archive a Twitter account yourself.

Yahoo includes the following paragraph in their terms:

> No Right of Survivorship and Non-Transferability. You agree that your Yahoo! account is non-transferable and any rights to your Yahoo! ID or contents within your account terminate upon your death. Upon receipt of a copy of a death certificate, your account may be terminated and all contents therein permanently deleted.

Yahoo takes a harsh stance on death, but the good news is that they will not take this action without the receipt of a death certificate. It's possible for you to ask your digital executor to archive your Yahoo account contents before presenting Yahoo with a death certificate.

YouTube doesn't specifically list their policies on death in their terms, but they do have an established policy, which requires your heir to provide a death certificate and documents giving them power of attorney over the YouTube account.

> If an individual has passed away and you need access to the content of his or her YouTube account, please fax or mail us the following information:

> 1. Your full name and contact information, including a verifiable email address.

2. The YouTube account name of the individual who passed away.

3. A copy of the death certificate of the deceased.

4. A copy of the document that gives you Power of Attorney over the YouTube account.

5. If you are the parent of the individual, please send us a copy of the Birth Certificate if the YouTube account owner was under the age of 18. In this case, Power of Attorney is not required.

Now that you've added all of your social accounts, you're almost done with the inventory. Next up we'll talk about the accounts you use to manage and spend your money.

✔ Take Action   *Wishes*

Now that we've covered your options, and discussed what you can legally request, it's time to document your wishes. Record your instructions and recipients in your inventory.

ASSET		ACCESS			WISHES	
Name	**Contents**	**Location**	**User Name**	**Password**	**Instructions**	**Recipient**
Facebook	Messages, Photos	www.facebook.com	joe.smith@email.com	cobraB!tes!	Memorialize	None
Twitter	Tweets	www.twitter.com/joe	Joe	JOein140	Post a final message	Bob Smith
Flickr	Photos	www.flickr.com/photos/15140142@N03	Joe_Smith	Sh0tsOjoe	Archive	Paul Smith
MySpace	Some photos, old messages	www.myspace.com/joerocks	Joerocks	My5p@c3	Delete	Bob Smith

Remember, we have an inventory template available at **www.yourdigitalafterlife.com/resources**.

CHAPTER 14

FINANCE AND COMMERCE

If you're like many other Internet users, you manage all sorts of financial information online. Whether it's buying, selling, or simply monitoring balances, you are likely to have several different online accounts to help. Chances are high that at least some of these accounts are connected to your bank accounts or credit cards. While your wealth is real property and will be handled by your estate plan, it's important to consider the online components of it in your digital estate plan. If you don't, the conveniences you enjoy transacting business online could become a real hassle for your executors and heirs.

Perhaps you receive your mortgage statement via email and make payments completely online. Of course, your heirs would know that you have a mortgage, but they may have no idea how to pay it. Estate planners used to count on statements showing up in the mail to alert them to accounts and provide contact information. But that's not the case anymore.

You may also earn revenue online through a site like eBay or an affiliate program. These types of accounts are managed solely online without the option for paper statements. Make sure your digital executor understands how you receive this revenue and can take the appropriate action.

In either of these situations, it will be much easier if your digital executor has your account credentials. But the goal is about more than convenience, it's about security. Let's consider another scenario: If you use a PayPal account, it's probably connected to your credit card or bank accounts and set up so that you can transfer funds to and from these accounts. To do this all you need is your PayPal user name and password, which can be easily reset if someone has the user name and password to your email account. Think about this when you select heirs and leave instructions for your digital executors. Remember that even a trusted, and technically savvy, person could be tempted to use their access inappropriately if they're strapped for cash. It's probably not a good idea to make them responsible for your financial security, so don't tempt them.

As you can probably imagine now, there are lots of complexities and interrelationships with online commerce. And there's no advice that's right for everyone. We're going to talk about giving access to your digital executor and other heirs, when that makes sense, and some pitfalls to avoid. Consider these issues and consult with an attorney or estate planner if you have specific concerns. After all, we're talking about real money here.

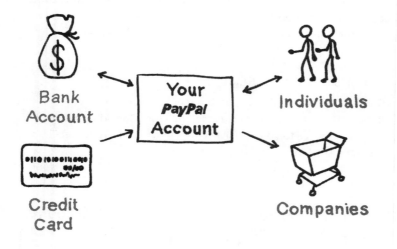

Services like PayPal are tightly integrated with many of your key financial accounts.

Awareness

It's a good idea to make your legal executor aware of any online dealings that involve your finances. And with the way commerce exists today, there are probably several types of dealings. We can think of them in terms of online accounts that help you manage your money, spend your money, and in some cases, make money for you.

Management Accounts

There are all sorts of accounts you may have to help manage your money. You might use a service like **Mint.com** or online banking provided by nearly every bank these days. You might also have online accounts that help you manage your 401k, health savings account, or other investments. Access to these accounts needs to be tightly controlled and should be recorded in your inventory. Remember, however, the disposition of these assets will be controlled by your legal will or by beneficiary designations. If you don't have a will, these assets will pass to your beneficiaries in accordance with the laws of either the state where the property is located or the state where you live. Simply including the online access for these accounts in your digital estate plan does not actually designate the disposition of the real value in the account. It does not say who gets the money; it simply makes your digital executor aware of the account and how to access it. This is important, however, so that action can be taken to protect the financial value of the account from online risks.

Email Is the Master Key

Remember that email is one of the master keys to your digital assets. That's true for financial accounts too. Consider that who-ever has access to your email account may also have the ability to reset the password for these accounts.

Online services like Mint.com help manage many of your financial accounts. Access to these accounts can be a treasure trove of information to your digital executor—or people with nefarious intentions.

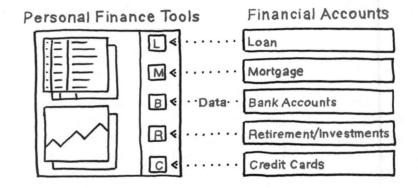

Online Purchases

There is no shortage of websites ready and willing to take your money. Everything from bill payment to shopping to subscription services is available online. Many of these may seem insignificant, but they are avenues through which money can leave your bank accounts. Make sure your digital executor is aware of them so he or she can take the necessary steps.

Many of these accounts are now linked directly to your checking account (see illustration on page 151). PayPal is one such service that allows you to pay for items at multiple sites and have the payments drafted directly from your account. These types of interconnected accounts are especially important to include in your inventory, as access to them provides direct access to your bank accounts.

You should also consider services that automatically renew at certain intervals. This includes news services, magazines, organization memberships, and any other content that you pay for online. The conveniences of auto-renewal could cause the account to remain active long after you need it. Making your digital executor aware of these is important; otherwise it might take several months for them to realize that purchases are recurring.

Online Earnings

You may even use the Internet to make money. Good for you. Chances are you utilize an affiliate program, receive advertising revenue from your website, or maybe you have an online store. In all of these cases you need to make special considerations for these accounts. Many of these have no offline component and could easily be overlooked. Ensure that this information is included in your inventory, or that these items are handled elsewhere, like your legal will or other arrangements.

 # Take Action   *Awareness*

Hopefully you found all of your financial accounts, or at least the important ones. Record the name and content of all your online accounts in your inventory.

ASSET		ACCESS			WISHES	
Name	Contents	Location	User Name	Password	Instructions	Heir
Zappos	Shopping					
eBay	Various items I'm selling					
Bank of America	Online banking, billpay					
Amazon Affiliate	Revenue from link sharing on my site					

Remember, we have an inventory template available at **www.yourdigitalafterlife.com/resources**.

Access

For most of these accounts, all you need to provide is a user name and password. Some accounts, however, have additional verification codes and questions. For instance, your online banking might ask you to enter your father's middle name or the city of your birth to verify your identity. It might be useful to include this information as well, but you'll need to consider it on a case-by-case basis as services vary widely in how they handle this.

For some accounts you may decide that you do not wish to leave the credentials with anyone. This can be appropriate for online banking and other accounts where these issues can be settled offline. You should, however, leave credentials for the accounts like PayPal where the only way to work with them is online. If you don't, there's a chance that your digital executor will never gain access even if they need to settle an account on your behalf.

 # Take Action   *Access*

List the location, user name, and passwords of your financial accounts.

ASSET		ACCESS			WISHES	
Name	**Contents**	**Location**	**User Name**	**Password**	**Instructions**	**Heir**
Zappos	Shopping	www.zappos.com	joe.smith@email.com	BuyJ03stuFF		
eBay	Various items I'm selling	www.ebay.com	JoeSells	BuyJ03stuFF		
Bank of America	Online banking, billpay	www.bankofamerica.com	Joe_Smith	bankOnjO3		
Amazon Affiliate	Revenue from link sharing on my site	www.amazon.com	Joerocks	joe!ndaJungl3		

Remember, we have an inventory template available at **www.yourdigitalafterlife.com/resources**.

Wishes

Next, record your wishes for each account. Keep in mind that your legal will dictates what will happen to your wealth and we're just talking about the accounts that help you manage it. Unlike other assets, you have a few basic options: Delete it, do nothing, or pass it to someone else.

Delete It

Deletion is the best option for accounts that you no longer need or that can be settled offline. In many cases you won't even need the credentials of an account to close it, but simply proof of death. We recommend that you instruct your digital executor to close all accounts that won't be needed after your death.

Do Nothing

Doing nothing is generally undesirable with this type of account, because all of your finances should be settled after your death and leaving an account open could put it at risk of unauthorized access. If this account is shared between multiple people, leaving it alone might be okay as long as the others have the necessary information. Even if you choose to do nothing with an account, you should consider leaving the access information for your digital executor. A situation might arise where they require access.

Pass It to Someone

Rarely is transferring ownership a viable option for financial accounts, unless you receive some sort of online revenue. Perhaps you run an online store or are an active eBay user and would like someone to continue the business. While you'll want to make legally binding arrangements in this situation, sharing the access information could be useful to keeping your business or other revenue stream running.

Heirs

Access to these accounts should be restricted to people who need to know, because of their connection to real property. Open access for everyone can be detrimental to the legal settlement of your estate.

For simplicity and security, it makes sense to provide this information only to your legal representatives. If you need to share it with others, consider the implications of doing so and remember that fewer are probably better.

Other Accounts

We know that you have many more accounts than what we've covered here: online services, websites, and mobile services; the list goes on and on. Listing all of them isn't necessary, but some of them could be very important to you. Make sure that all your important accounts are recorded in your inventory. Appendix A contains information about finding important accounts that may be of help to you.

At this point we've discussed the four basic types of digital assets: computers and devices, email, social websites, and financial accounts. If you followed along, you now have your own inventory, complete with access information, heirs, and wishes. Now it's time to turn that inventory into a plan. So turn the page.

✔ Take Action   *Wishes*

List the instructions and heirs for each account.

ASSET		ACCESS			WISHES	
Name	**Contents**	**Location**	**User Name**	**Password**	**Instructions**	**Heir**
Zappos	Shopping	www.zappos.com	joe.smith@email.com	BuyJ03stuFF	Delete	None
eBay	Various items I'm selling	www.ebay.com	JoeSells	BuyJ03stuFF	Pass	Bob Smith
Bank of America	Online banking, billpay	www.bankofamerica.com	Joe_Smith	bankOnjO3	Do nothing	
Amazon Affiliate	Revenue from link sharing on my site	www.amazon.com	Joerocks	joe!ndaJungl3	Pass	Paul Smith

Remember, we have an inventory template available at **www.yourdigitalafterlife.com/resources**.

CHAPTER 15

CREATE YOUR PLAN

Congratulations! You deserve a pat on the back. You now have an inventory of your digital assets, complete with your instructions and wishes. That's an undertaking in itself.

In fact, that work was essential, but now you need to ensure that your inventory and instructions are carried out. Since you won't be there to push the buttons, you'll need a person or service to do it for you. And for that, you need a plan. Your plan will have four basic parts:

1. Storage—a place to keep your inventory and instructions

2. Trigger—an event that releases your plan from storage

3. Digital executor—a person or service to distribute or delete your assets

4. Heirs—the people who receive your assets

Wills and Estate Plans

It's tempting to simply put user names and passwords in your will, but that's actually a bad idea. After your will is read it becomes a public record and anyone, not just your heirs, can have access to it.

There are digital estate services that can help with all parts of the process. Generally speaking, all services provide you with storage and a trigger and many also serve as a digital executor for you. You can also choose to do more of the work yourself. You could utilize a posthumous email service and craft emails to heirs. You could also take the entire process offline, using anything from a safe deposit box to a secret location in your home.

The options are limitless, but you'll want to pick the one that's best for your situation. We encourage you to think through the entire process systematically, from storage to heir, before making a decision. Let's cover a few scenarios now, and then we'll talk about the issues you should consider before making a final decision.

Digital Estate Services

Digital estate services can make this process really easy for you and your heirs. Most of them have free versions that are quite useful, with additional services available for a fee. Appendix C contains an index of digital afterlife services.

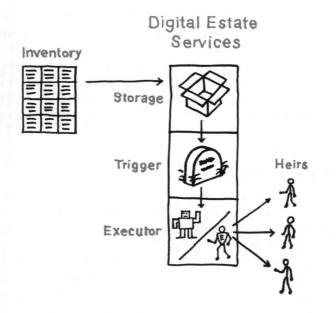

Storage

With this option, all the items in your inventory are stored on servers owned by the digital estate service. You place them there by creating an account with the service and inputting the information via a web browser. Your information is kept there until your trigger is activated.

Password Vaults

Remember that having a list of your user names and passwords will help you while you're alive too. DataInherit has an iPhone app that gives you quick access to your passwords, which are stored in their secure data center.

Trigger

The trigger for each service varies slightly, offering different degrees of protection for your information. Legacy Locker, for example, requires that two verifiers whom you select must inform them of your death and then provide a certified copy of your death certificate before your assets will be released. Entrustet also requires a copy of your death certificate, but members of their team contact local health records offices before releasing your information. Another option, DataInherit, provides you with a 36-character access code, which you can access at anytime, that you print and provide to a trusted person. Once the code has been entered, a waiting period, specified by you, begins and DataInherit will attempt to contact you in that time. If they do not hear from you, your information is released after the waiting period ends.*

Digital Executor

We said earlier that your digital executor is the person who distributes or deletes your digital assets. Any other wishes you have will be carried out by an heir. Most services will deliver your information directly to your heirs via email. One service, Entrustet, asks that you choose a real person as your digital executor. Once the Entrustet staff verifies that you have passed, your digital executor will be able to send your information to heirs when the time is right. This is another manual safeguard to ensure alignment with your offline estate plan.

Posthumous Email Services

Posthumous email services send out messages you have written in advance and designated to be delivered upon your death. Like digital estate services, these provide a trigger to initiate their services. If you choose to craft email messages with user names and passwords, these services could also be used as storage for your inventory and even act as your digital executor. This method may require more work on your part and is arguably less secure, but it affords you an

---

*Throughout this chapter we'll reference different online services and explain how they work. We've made every effort to ensure that these descriptions are correct at the time of publication, but they could change in the future.

opportunity to write each message individually. That could allow you to write personal messages in addition to sharing user names and passwords. Appendix C contains a list of these services.

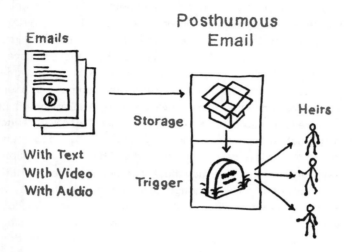

Storage

You may use a posthumous email service as storage for your inventory. Instead of storing sets of assets and associating them with a heir, you store email messages addressed to a heir. To add your inventory and assets to an email service, you'll need to write an email for each heir. In that email you'll likely include a short message, followed by a list of user names, passwords, and wishes.

You also may store your inventory elsewhere and use the email service to inform a live digital executor about how to access it. This would allow you to choose a convenient and updatable inventory management scheme that you make your digital executor aware of.

A Note on Instructions

Be sure to write specific and detailed instructions. You won't be there to clarify your intentions and your heirs might be distraught if they can't carry out your final wishes.

Trigger

With the wide array of email services comes a good deal of variability in trigger mechanisms. The triggers used for email services generally rely on your lack of response or a group of notifiers to confirm your death. One service, **ifidie.org**, will send you an email and SMS (text message) every two weeks. Not receiving a response from you, they ask a group of "keyholders" (whom you specify) whether you have died before sending your messages. That might not be a good idea if you prefer to take long vacations away from your computer or phone. **GreatGoodbye.com** relies on an activation code, like DataInherit, that you can give to a trusted person. Another service, **DeadMansSwitch. net**, is just that—a dead man's switch. If you fail to respond to three of their emails they will release your information. These trigger options are significantly less reliable than those that require a death certificate and may not be reliable enough for your purposes. With any of the services that require you to respond to messages from time to time to assure that you're alive and well, consider that those could be erroneously activated if you're in the hospital or on an extended vacation. So if you like to check out periodically, these might not be for you.

Digital Executor

With posthumous email services, the role of digital executor can either be played by the service or by an individual who receives the email. The service can, in effect, act as the digital executor if you craft specific emails to all your heirs that contain the credentials. However no additional oversight or account deletion services are provided. If that's something you need, you may want to appoint a live executor and use the service to email them the information needed to do their job.

Do-It-Yourself Methods

You might prefer to devise your own method of passing your inventory and instructions. For these you'll need to devise your own storage, trigger, and executor options.

Storage

The first step in planning is to decide where your instructions will be stored. Storing them on your personal computer is problematic unless you back up to a secure, accessible location. Hard drives can easily fail and your plan would be subject to all the device access issues we discussed in Chapter 8, Your Legacy at Risk. That said, you can store your information anywhere you like, as long as your digital executor knows about it or your trigger will deliver it to them.

Some ideas:

- Store it as a spreadsheet on your computer and back it up.
- Store it as a spreadsheet on your computer, and print it out and store it with your legal will (but not as a legal part of your will).
- Store it as a spreadsheet on a thumb drive and keep it in a home safe or safe deposit box,
- Send yourself an email for each account to a web-based email account. Store the emails in a folder and send email to yourself each time you change or add an account.

Trigger

The simplest do-it-yourself trigger is allowing your digital executor to take action when the time is right. If you chose to print out your inventory and instructions, you could also place it in a secure location that your digital executor would only receive access to upon your death. You might store it in your home lockbox so you have control of it until you pass, and provide your digital executor with a key to open the box so they can access it later. You could even provide access in your legal will by bequeathing the contents of a safe deposit box to your digital executor.

Digital Executor

The key to a manual process is the person you choose to serve as your digital executor. That person will receive your inventory and instructions and then take action. Keep in mind that your digital executor will have access to all the accounts in your inventory until they pass them to the appropriate person. As such, you should consider a few things when selecting a digital executor. We like to say it boils down to trust, distance, and capability.

Trust

Considering that you will be granting your passwords to this individual and they'll have unfettered access to your digital assets, trust is essential. Remember that there is nothing to stop them from taking action when the time is not yet right. You'll want to trust that they will carry out your wishes and won't abuse their power.

Distance

Select someone who has an appropriate distance from you. If you're asking for some things to be deleted, a friend might be better, as a close family member might be clinging to everything about you and feel unable to press the delete button. Conversely, you may have highly sensitive content that you only want your close family to deal with. Selecting two digital executors might also afford the appropriate distance for your situation.

Capability

With all the technical details you've put in your inventory document, you can imagine that a technically minded person is best for the job.

Issues

So now that you understand the options, let's talk about the issues. By understanding these issues, and which options suffer from them, you'll be able to make an informed decision about your plan.

Security

Let's start by remembering the reason you have user names and passwords to begin with—security. You want to make sure that your digital assets are secure both before and after you pass away. Ideally no one would know your passwords until you pass away, and then only your digital executor and specific heirs should have access.

Simply put, by writing your password down anywhere, you make it less secure. It's possible for someone who knows where your plan is located to steal your passwords, if it's not properly secured. If security is highly important to you, a digital afterlife service might be the best option. Do-it-yourself methods will also work, but with a specific focus on physical security.

Updatability

There are a number of reasons why you want to update your plan. You'll inevitably add new accounts or perhaps you'll go through some sort of life event that makes you reconsider your wishes. Perhaps you change your password often and need an easy way to update your inventory. In all of these cases, consider how often you may need to update your plan. If you'll need to do so frequently, you need a solution that allows you to update quickly. A digital afterlife service might be best for that, or a separate email account to which you can fire off a quick email. Needless to say, a printed document in a safe deposit box probably won't work well.

Number of Heirs

On your inventory sheet you may have many things going to the same person or you may have lots of different people. As you add more heirs your plan will become complex. Think for a moment about all the effort that one digital executor will need to go through to pass accounts to several different people. In those situations, a service might be the right option. Email or do-it-yourself options might make sense for a smaller, less complex plan.

Your Age

We know that death can come at any time, but as you grow older death becomes more imminent. Consider how long your plan will remain in storage before you need it. Additionally, some services cost money. Younger people may find it wasteful to spend money for something they may not need for many decades.

Your Ability

Whatever solution you choose is going to take some time, but you might be able to save some by using a service. Those teams have worked hard to make the process as quick and seamless as possible for you and your digital executors. If you're short on time or would rather not take on the task of building your own plan, a service might be the right option.

Trigger Reliability

The goal with a trigger is to ensure that your plan remains in storage until the moment it's needed. This keeps your accounts secure while you're alive. With the array of trigger options, you'll want to consider this carefully. If you can trust one person to set the plan into action, then a do-it-yourself method or the 36-character password from DataInherit might be the right option. If you prefer safety in numbers, services that utilize a group of trusted notifiers may be right for you. Even so, you might prefer the most secure option, which requires a death certificate. Remember that as you make this more secure you increase the amount of work expected from your survivors. You'll want to balance this with the reliability you prefer.

How Do I Decide?

Ultimately, you need to balance all of these issues; there is no one-size-fits-all solution. With that in mind, let's consider this from another angle. For each type we've outlined the type of person who will be best served by that particular plan. Pick the list of traits that most closely matches your situation and that's probably the right option for you.

Digital Estate Services

Good for people who want someone to help them and who:

- Have a basic understanding of computers but don't understand how to plan
- Want the most stringent third-party verification process, often including death certificates

- Want a guide
- Might be willing to spend money, but don't have a lot of time
- Want an automated digital executor
- Have one or many recipients
- Have passwords that change frequently
- Open new accounts often

Posthumous Email

Good for people who want a highly personalized service and who:

- Have a basic understanding of computers and understand how to make a plan
- Don't mind a slightly less stringent third-party verification process and don't need the additional legal protection of a death certificate
- Want some of the benefits of a digital service, but want more flexibility to create their own plan
- Might be willing to spend money and are willing to put some time into the issue
- Don't want to put everything in the hands of one person
- Have one or many recipients
- Have passwords that don't change that often
- Don't open new accounts often

Do-It-Yourself Method

Good for people who want to make up their own simple plan and who:

- Understand computers and how to make a plan
- Want to design their own verification process that won't include a death certificate
- Are the do-it-yourself type
- Don't want to spend any money, but have time to figure out a plan
- Have a live digital executor whom they trust completely

- Have either a simple plan or the organization to manage a complex plan
- Can design something to accommodate the frequency with which they create new accounts and change passwords

Adding Legal Weight

Throughout this section we have covered various aspects of the law. You may want to ensure that your digital legacy has some sort of legal protection. At this time, the law has not caught up with our new digital society. Following your death the only person with any legal authority is the legal executor of your estate, as defined in your will. Consider making that person your digital executor as well and include reference to your digital estate plan in your will. In this way, the probate court will authorize and enable your digital executor to take the appropriate action in relation to your accounts. You should, however, make sure that you're in compliance with the terms for any particular account.

Remember, we can't provide legal advice, nor do we intend to. If you're concerned about adding legal weight, be sure to consult your attorney.

What's Next?

Congratulations, you now have a plan to secure your digital legacy. Doesn't that feel good? Your next step is to set it into action. Go sign up for a service or write instructions for your digital executor and put your trigger in place.

Once you do that you're free to enjoy life with the peace of mind that you've made things a little easier for your heirs. Over time, you should do a few things: Revisit your plan every six months or so to ensure it's up-to-date. Add any new accounts, remove old ones, and adjust heirs as needed. Get into the habit of doing your "account house-keeping" and keeping things organized. It will inevitably help you and your heirs.

The nice thing is that your inventory will serve as a repository of access for you for all the years of your life. Computer crashes, hard drive failures, or poor memory will no longer cause you to misplace your access to your necessary websites and accounts.

Keep an eye on the digital afterlife industry for new technologies and policies. The Web of five years ago is completely different than the Web of today. Best practices for securing your digital identity will inevitably change and you'll want to adjust your plan accordingly. But all your work won't be in vain—the organization and planning you put into this process will serve as a strong foundation for revising your plans.

EPILOGUE

The Future of Digital Death

During our research over the last several years, we've had a few "aha" moments. Along the way we realized that the widespread preservation of personal digital content, and the introduction of technology into the experience of death, would have a significant impact on society. Now that you've learned about the digital afterlife, and have taken steps to secure your own, we thought it would be a good time to share some of these thoughts with you. So if you'll pardon the loose association of topics, you'll get a glimpse of our latest thinking and perhaps what's coming next in this arena.

The Burden of the Past

As we do a better job of storing digital things, it's worth considering the impact it will have on the future. Today, antique stores are full of failed family heirlooms. The things that were once a meaningful part of someone's life are no longer meaningful to their heirs, and they have been disposed of. It's unfortunate, but that's the reality of physical things. After some time you just have to part ways with most things. But despite the small space that digital things take up, this could be the case for them as well. We can't help but wonder how long individuals and companies will continue to maintain the content of the deceased.

Let's look at Facebook as an example. They agree to memorialize a profile after its owner passes away. But the number of memorialized profiles will grow over time. Facebook's 500 million members represent 8 percent of the world's 6.2 billion people. What happens over decades? Do they continue to memorialize accounts forever? If they do, the burden of the past will weigh heavily on them in the future. Perhaps they'll eventually retire them? But performing a mass deletion in a hundred years might become akin to Ellis Island deleting immigration records from the 1800s.

This issue also plays out on a personal level. Consider the data that you might leave behind. In the future it will probably be considered a relatively small amount, but it may be hard to sort through and gain any value from it. We hope that the computers of the future will become better at sense making and it won't be an issue at all.

We're not sure what will happen here, but the burden of the past is worth considering. Perhaps we should take more care in the present to specify the most important things in our lives, to avoid being a burden in the future? Or perhaps we should let life take its course and join countless others in the forgotten past?

The Internet does have a limited, short-term memory. Stored there will be an incalculable amount of data that is disconnected and left behind, unwanted by users. Included in this will be abandoned accounts and profiles, haunting the Internet like ghosts from the past that slowly decay over time.

The Creation of Standards

Death is handled differently at every site that requires you to have an account. We don't think that's good enough. We believe there's a distinct need to create universal policies that can be used across multiple websites. Ideally those standards would propose consistent procedures and language, creating a pattern that users will recognize and accept. If you were asked to specify an heir (or an executor) for every account you have, without creating an additional plan, more people would consider this important issue.

Universal policies would need to be fair to everyone involved, making sure to honor the deceased and respect their families, yet still remain open so that the greater community can learn from them. It's a balance between privacy and value in the future. If the family of Charles Dickens had attempted to hide his work away, we would still know of him today, because his work was in print. With a multitude of printed copies available it would have been impossible for his family to dispose of all of them. But the work of bloggers and other online publishers is usually stored as one copy on one server that's one click away from deletion. Despite the honorable and effective efforts of the Internet Archive, it's too easy for a website to disappear without a trace. It's not possible for the Internet Archive to store the entire Web. In cases where they can't archive a site, either because of space constraints or being denied permission from the site's owner, deleted content is gone from the world.

We're anxious to see what progress will be made in the coming years—and on which of these issues. Will standardization come from the service providers? Or will it be a government initiative? Or better yet, how about a working group of experts who craft the policy and encourage adoption?

The Future of Cultural Research

Researchers have studied identity and communication for decades, if not longer. One of the core challenges to their research is that extensive observation, note taking, and even participation was required to understand communication. With the huge set of data that resides on the Web, we have the opportunity to understand communication in new ways. Researchers are studying the content at sites like Facebook and Twitter, and one day they might do the same thing to understand the culture and values of our generation. For this to happen, we'll need computing power and algorithms to sift through the content, to make sense of it. We'll also need a way to make data anonymous to protect the creator. Researchers are already hard at work on both and it's only a matter of time before we learn more and more from what we share digitally.

Connected Cemeteries

When you think of the cemetery you probably think of a solemn, reverent place that's not subject to the changes we've seen in technology over the last several years. We had similar thoughts until we learned of the role mobile devices are playing. We've read stories about mobile devices being placed on the deceased in their caskets. And as they're put to rest, friends and family are texting their last goodbyes. Others go so far as to leave the deceased's mobile services active, so they can continue to hear their voicemail greeting. In fact, some keep paying the bill for months so they can, for a moment, feel their loved one's presence. But that's only the beginning of technology in the cemetery.

Several companies already sell digital headstones and digital cemetery experiences. One company, Rosetta Stone, offers microchips for headstones (**personalRosettaStone.com**, not the software for learning foreign languages). Each chip can communicate up to 1,000 words and an image to an NFC-RFID–enabled mobile device. Information can also be accessed by visiting the URL inscribed on the device. Cemeteries provide loved ones with an in-person experience; the Internet offers rich online memorials. Companies like Rosetta Stone seek to link the two types of experiences. Fascinating stuff.

The challenge that these companies face will be the mismatch between the permanence of headstones with the transient and evolutionary nature of technology. Our computers tend to last three to five years, our mobile phones 18 months. How can a digital product fixed to a headstone possibly last?

Experiencing the Past

One of the reasons we create photo albums is to create a vision of the past for the future. Before photos all we had was the written word and the occasional painting, and before that stories that were passed orally between generations. All these things still happen today and there's absolutely nothing wrong with that. Consider for a moment how we could experience the past if we could interpret the entirety of your digital content after you're gone. Perhaps we could analyze your emails, tweets, and Facebook posts to understand your beliefs and opinions on certain issues. Perhaps your blog could be used to determine tone and vocabulary. We could even look to photos and videos to understand appearance and gestures. And a look at your various social networking profiles and emails could tell us about your friends and connections.

With all that data, what could we do? Let's consider what's being done today. Researchers at Carnegie Mellon University have developed the Synthetic Interview. It's a multimedia experience that uses the writings of historical figures like Abraham Lincoln to construct a video representation of him that responds to questions. Thus far their work requires an actor for a video shoot and they restrict their work to historical accuracy. By using the text to infer how the interviewee might respond they've created a historical product that's of great interest to museums.

Imagine if that same technology could be applied to all your digital content. Some artificial intelligence engine could rifle through the content and base its personality and responses on you. That's exactly what the Bina48 robot does. Bina48 is an advanced humanoid robot located at the Terasem Movement Foundation in Bristol, Vermont. Bina48's personality is modeled from a real person, who spent hours speaking to the robot, instilling her experience and vocabulary. The robot is also connected to the Internet so she can gain additional understanding. Today interviews with Bina48 aren't very conversational, but it's clear that she is improving in understanding and learning over time.

With advancements like these it's likely that we'll be able to construct similar representations of an individual based on his or her online content. Perhaps those lifeloggers have the right idea. With a lifetime's worth of recordings, their humanoid robots might be the most accurate and responsive ones yet. We're not sure how they're planning to use their data, but it's an interesting idea to consider.

Imagine that you had a humanoid robot that would pick up for you after you pass away. It would certainly change the way we experience the past. Imagine, instead of reading about and looking at photos of Grandpa, you could sit down and ask him a few questions. These representations might convey some of his wisdom and life experiences, and in a way, his influence and presence in your life.

Some Parting Thoughts

Now that you have an understanding of digital assets and a plan for passing them along after you die, you're equipped for the future. Without a doubt, we're going to see changes in this space, due partly to an increasing awareness of digital death and legacy issues and partly to the evolving nature of technology. Based on current trends and some things we already see in the works, a few things are certain:

- Technology will continue advancing at a record-breaking pace. Our devices will become more powerful, more ubiquitous, and smaller. That's going to continue fueling the content explosion on the Web.

- A new generation of Digital Natives will enter adulthood and begin (well, really continue) creating content at an unprecedented rate.

- The law will catch up with the times and eventually create some certainty about digital assets. It might take a landmark court case, or a heightened awareness of the issue, but we'll get there.

- Services that host digital content will become even more aware of the importance of the content they host and its value to users and their heirs. We can only hope that will evolve into policies that are in the best interest of users.

Today, we're just beginning this discussion and this book is just that: a beginning. It's our hope that it will serve as a call to action for greater dialogue about this subject. In thirty years, perhaps we won't need a book about digital death and legacy issues. Hopefully the ideas, policies, and cultural norms will become institutionalized in our society.

But for now, we're hopeful that this book is helpful to you in securing your digital content for posterity. So back up your stuff, make your plan, and stick to it. Be sure to revisit your plan every once in a while, as the Internet changes fast. With your legacy on the line, you'll want to stay on top of it.

Do it for yourself, for your loved ones, and for posterity. Enjoy the peace of mind that your treasured assets will have a digital afterlife and be secured for generations to come.

APPENDIX

A. Finding Forgotten Accounts

With an increasing number of websites requiring you to create an account, it's likely that you have a large number of them—probably more than you realize. Some of these might not be important to you, but others could contain rich content that you've created and since forgotten about. Here are a few tips for rediscovering forgotten accounts.

Check Your Web Browser

As the portal through which you access most online content, your Web browser is full of information about your online interactions. A quick look at your bookmarks or browser history will show some of the sites you frequent. Chances are some of them are sites you log in to access. If you save passwords in your browser, you can also look to your saved password lists for this information.

Firefox for Windows or Mac

Mac users go to the Firefox menu > Preferences. PC users go to the Tools menu > Options. Click the Security tab. The Saved Passwords button brings up a list of sites where you have a stored password.

There are add-ons that allow you to export your saved passwords. Visit **www.yourdigitalafterlife.com/resources** to learn about your options.

Safari or Chrome for Mac

Go to the Applications folder > Utilities and open Keychain Access. Choose Passwords to see a list of saved passwords from your browser.

Chrome for Windows

Go to the Tools menu > Options > Minor Tweaks tab. In the Passwords section, click the Show saved passwords button.

Internet Explorer for Windows

There are several options, too many to mention here. Visit **www. yourdigitalafterlife.com/resources** to learn more.

Check Your Email

When you sign up for an online account an email is often sent to you for verification. Sometimes these emails include your user name and/or password, but at the very least they provide a record that you created an account. That can be very useful for discovering accounts you've forgotten about.

If you save your old emails, you can use your email client's search tool to find these messages. Give it a try using search terms like *account, user name*, *password*, and *confirm*.

In the future, consider saving all your account emails in a folder when they arrive. This could become a good reference for you, and a great directory of your accounts for your survivors, in case you haven't thoroughly documented your online accounts elsewhere.

B. Tools for Archiving Social Websites

Many of the social websites you use probably have your content locked up in some way. These products and services can help you manage and/or archive your content so you can back it up properly. We don't endorse these tools so use at your own risk. Please visit **www.yourdigitalafterlife.com/resources** for the most up to date information.

Multiple Accounts

Backupify
www.backupify.com

Socialware Sync
sync.socialware.com

Blogs

BlogBackupr
blogbackupr.com

Facebook

1000Memories
1000memories.com
www.facebook.com/apps/application.php?id=130678670286090

ArchiveFacebook

addons.mozilla.org/en-US/firefox/addon/13993

Facebook Download

Facebook allows you to download your profile information, Wall posts, photos, videos and messages in a zipped archive. All you have to do is visit your Account Settings and click "Download Your Information."

SocialSafe

www.socialsafe.net

Flickr

Downloadr

flickrdownloadr.codeplex.com

FlickrEdit

sunkencity.org/flickredit

Flickr Backup

sourceforge.net/projects/flickrbackup

Twitter

BackupMyTweets

backupmytweets.com

Tweetake

tweetake.com

TweetBackup

tweetbackup.com

Tweetscan

www.tweetscan.com

It's worth noting that Twitter has a policy for deceased users that allows your next-of-kin to obtain an archived copy of your public tweets upon providing proper documentation of your passing.

LinkedIn

You can use the built-in LinkedIn functionality to export your contacts.

www.linkedin.com/addressBookExport

C. Index of Digital Afterlife Services

Throughout this book we mention several digital afterlife services. Here's a list of all of the ones we know about at the time of publication. Visit **www.yourdigitalafterlife.com/resources** for the latest list.

Digital Estate Planning and Posthumous Email Services

These services can be used to help you set your digital estate plan into motion.

AssetLock
www.assetlock.net
Provides digital estate planning services.

Bcelebrated
www.bcelebrated.com
Provides online memorials and posthumous email services.

DataInherit
www.datainherit.com
Provides digital estate planning services.

Dead Man's Switch
www.deadmansswitch.net
Provides posthumous email services.

Death Switch
deathswitch.com
Provides posthumous email services.

Entrustet
www.entrustet.com
Provides digital estate planning services.

Estate++
www.estateplusplus.com
Provides digital estate planning services.

Executor's Resource
www.executorsresource.com
Provides digital estate planning services.

The Estate Vault
www.estatevault.com
Provides digital estate planning services.

GreatGoodbye
greatgoodbye.com
Provides posthumous email services.

if i die.org
ifidie.org
Provides posthumous email services.

Legacy Locker
www.legacylocker.com
Provides digital estate planning and posthumous email services.

MentoMori
mentomori.com
Provides digital estate planning and posthumous email services.

My Digital Afterlife
www.mydigitalafterlife.com
Provides digital estate planning and posthumous email services.

My Web Will
www.mywebwill.com
Provides digital estate planning services.

My Wonderful Life
www.mywonderfullife.com
Provides posthumous email services.

Slightly Morbid
www.slightlymorbid.com
Provides posthumous email services.

VitalLock
vitallock.com
Provides posthumous email services.

Xsen.de
xsen.de
Provides digital estate planning and posthumous email services.

Online Memorial Services

You can use these services to create a memorial for a loved one, or in some cases, yourself.

Bcelebrated
www.bcelebrated.com

1000Memories
1000memories.com

GoneTooSoon
www.gonetoosoon.org

Legacy.com
legacy.com

Lifestrand
www.lifestrand.net

Memorial Gardens
www.memorial-gardens.org

Memorial Matters
www.memorialmatters.com

Online Legacy/Permasite
www.online-legacy.com

People To Remember
people2remember.com

Remembered Forever
www.remembered-forever.org

Remembered Voices
rememberedvoices.com

RememberWell
www.rememberwell.net

SympathyTree
www.sympathytree.com

Tributes.com
tributes.com

D. Reading List

Here's a list of websites you can check out for more information.

The Digital Beyond
www.thedigitalbeyond.com
Written by the authors of this book, this blog sparked the idea for
Your Digital Afterlife.

Death and Digital Legacy
www.deathanddigitallegacy.com
This is a blog written by another digital death researcher, Adele
McAlear.

Digital Estate Planning
www.digitalestateplanning.com
This blog by Nathan Dosch, our legal reviewer for the book, digs into
the legal issues surrounding digital assets.

Wills, Trusts & Estates Professor Blog
lawprofessors.typepad.com/trusts_estates_prof/technology
This blog by Gerry Beyer explores the legal and estate planning
aspects of digital death.

Blogs from Digital Death Service Providers

While these blogs are from companies selling services, they all have
great content on the subject.

1000 Memories Blog
1000memories.com/blog

DataInherit Blog
datainherit.wordpress.com

Entrustet Blog
blog.entrustet.com

Legacy Locker Blog
blog.legacylocker.com

GLOSSARY

Cloud is a metaphor for the Internet.

Cloud computing is a paradigm shift in computing. Instead of applications being installed locally on a user's own computer, cloud-based applications are available to computers and other devices on demand via the Internet.

Cloud storage refers to computer files that are stored on the Internet. Photos on Flickr and videos on YouTube are examples of files stored in the cloud.

Data "myning" is a term coined by TrendWatching.com. A play on data mining, it's the act of users claiming the data on the Internet that belongs to them.

Digital executor is the person you appoint to handle your digital affairs after you die. He or she distributes your digital assets to the heirs whom you specify.

Digital Rights Management (DRM) is a generic term that refers to protections placed on digital content to limit its usage. Music downloaded from iTunes that can only be played by the person who purchased it is an example of DRM technology in use.

Domain name registration is the process of paying a registrar an annual fee to include your domain in DNS servers.

Domain Name System (DNS) is the system used to name computers on the Internet. DNS servers are used to translate human-readable domain names into numeric addresses.

Forced heirship is a legal term that refers to a situation in which laws dictate how assets are distributed to heirs. This is most prevalent in Islamic countries, but also occurs in other jurisdictions such as France, Japan and the State of Louisiana (USA).

Heir refers to the person(s) whom you specify as the recipient(s) of your property, digital or otherwise, after you die.

Internet Message Access Protocol (IMAP) is one of two popular email protocols in use on the Internet. Email accounts using IMAP often leave copies of email messages on the email server.

Internet Service Provider (ISP) is a company that provides customers with access to the Internet.

Lifestream is the chronological collection of content that chronicles your digital life.

Local storage, the opposite of cloud storage, refers to files stored in the same physical space as you. Files stored on computers and devices are stored locally.

Metadata is additional information attached to content that provides a further description of that content. Things like date, location, and filename might be typical metadata for a photograph.

National Strategy for Trusted Identities in Cyberspace (NSTIC) is an initiative of the White House and several US government agencies to address issues surrounding the protection of the identity of each party in an online transaction.

Near Field Communication-Radio Frequency Identification (NFC-RFID) NFC is a two-way communication technology based on RFID that shares information wirelessly between two nearby devices.

Nontransferable is a legal term that means you cannot transfer something, like your user name and password, to someone else. It is often used in terms of service agreements.

Nontransferability clause is the section of a terms of service agreement that states that the account in question is nontransferable.

Notifier is a general term for a person who notifies a digital estate service or posthumous email service of a user's death.

Post Office Protocol (POP3) is one of two popular email protocols in use on the Internet. Email accounts using POP3 often download copies of email messages and delete them from the email server.

Power of attorney is a legal term that means an individual has authorization to act on behalf of another person in legal or business matters.

Right of survivorship is a legal term that refers to what happens to jointly owned property in the event of one owner's death.

Short Message Service (SMS) is the technical name for short text messages sent between telephones.

Social Web refers to the set of websites that allow users to contribute content and connect with each other. This includes social networking sites, like Facebook, and social media sites, like YouTube.

Transmission Control Protocol/Internet Protocol (TCP/IP) describes the set of rules that computers follow when exchanging data on the Internet.

Terms of service is a legally binding contract between a business and its customers, for example, a web-based company and the users of its website. It often states who owns the content that a user uploads and sometimes dictates what happens to that content after the user's death.

Termination is the act of brining something to an end. In this book, it generally refers to the closing of an online account by the company and not the account holder.

Transferability is a legal term that refers to the ability to transfer property, such as an online account and its contents, from one person to another. It is usually used in the negative, i.e., nontransferability.

Trigger is an event that causes another event to take place. In this book, it refers to the mechanism used to determine that someone has died and then distribute their digital assets accordingly.

Tweet is a short, 140-character message sent using Twitter.

Uniform Resource Locator (URL) is an identifier that specifies where a resource is available and the mechanism for retrieving it. It usually refers to an address on the Web, e.g., http://www.yourdigitalafterlife.com.

Web 2.0 is another name for the *Social Web*. It refers collectively to websites that allow users to contribute content and connect with each other.

Web hosting is a service that affords customers the ability to make a website available on the Web.

From the Authors

Trust us, we never thought we would be the guys who study death. To many people it's considered a bit morbid. We get that. But we have a strong desire to highlight the change that is happening in our culture and raise awareness of digital death issues. We like to think of our work as helpful and aspirational.

As we researched this book, we found stories of individuals—some whose digital content was saved after their death and others whose assets are gone forever. These stories both saddened and inspired us. They were a call to action, to help people understand the complexities of a digital life and how to pass on their digital content after death. It's important for society to understand the opportunity of digital legacy, the challenges to fulfilling that opportunity, and the advancements we've seen thus far.

If one person's digital legacy is saved—or deleted, if that is their desire—because of our work, this book will be a success. If it helps spark a greater conversation about these issues, even better.

About Us

Since 2008, we have been researching and writing about the budding digital afterlife community. We first presented our research to a crowded room at the South By Southwest conference (SXSW) in 2009, and were immediately mentioned on NPR's "All Tech Considered."

We then created The Digital Beyond—**thedigitalbeyond.com**—as a think tank for digital death and legacy issues. The site has grown into the go-to source for digital afterlife information. The *New York Times*, *Obit* magazine, *Orlando Sentinel*, and the *Austin Chronicle* have mentioned The Digital Beyond and have consulted us on related stories. In November 2009, we appeared on CNN in a featured video story, "Planning Your Digital Afterlife." We returned to SXSW in 2010 to host another session called "Become Immortal: Understanding the Digital Afterlife."

John Romano

John works as an interaction designer, technology researcher, and cultural observer. His work centers on the mass adoption of digital tools and the ways they are changing how we interact with each other. When he isn't writing or speaking, he is designing websites, building stuff in the garage with his son, or riding his motorcycle. John holds a Bachelor of Environmental Design degree from the North Carolina State University College of Design.

Evan Carroll

Evan Carroll is an experience designer and researcher. His passion is observing how people interact with technology and using that insight to create user-centered products and services—a passion that led him to study the digital afterlife. In Evan's spare time, you'll find him pulling for the Tar Heels or escaping the digital world at the North Carolina coast. Evan holds a Bachelor of Science degree in Information Science and has completed additional graduate studies at UNC-Chapel Hill's School of Information and Library Science.

A word cloud created from the text of this book showing the relative frequency of key words.

INDEX